SHADES CAHABA

THE FIRST
100 YEARS

SHAWN WRIGHT

SHAWN WRIGHT

Birmingham, AL 35209

shawnwright.net

Book design by Shawn Wright

Author photo by Laurey Glenn

ISBN: 978-1-7355822-0-7

For Leigh, Aidan and Ethan

Contents

Preface

I GREW UP IN HOMEWOOD and have spent most of my life here. It wasn't the plan, but something kept me here.

I was born at South Highlands Infirmary, and my parents brought me to our home on the second floor of the East Glenwood Apartments. According to my parents, I would hold on to the crib's side and move it across the floor by jumping up and down. This story may be a parental exaggeration, but we soon moved to a house on Primrose Place to our downstairs neighbor's joy.

When I was old enough, I attended All-Saints Episcopal Preschool in a house behind the main church on Edgewood Boulevard. All-Saints offered primary school through second grade, and my parents kept me at All-Saints through first grade. During the spring, we moved to Kensington Road in the Mayfair section of Homewood. My parents decided to send me to a public school in the fall. I was no longer zoned for Edgewood Elementary; I would attend Shades Cahaba Elementary.

I spent the next four years at Shades Cahaba, followed by my younger brother, who attended five years. Years later, I would drive past the school and think back to what the hallways looked like, who my teachers were, and the fun I had with my friends.

I moved away to attend Auburn University with no plans to return and live in Birmingham. After graduation, I got my first job in town, then the second and so on. I started to put down roots, and other than five or six years where I lived on the southside of Birmingham, I have lived in Homewood. I have owned four homes here—in Edgewood, off Valley Avenue, in West Homewood, and finally Hollywood. I looked in other parts of Birmingham, but something kept calling me back.

The move to Hollywood was with a new wife and thoughts of raising a family. We quickly added two children, Aidan and Ethan, and they both attend Shades Cahaba Elementary. Ethan just finished fifth grade and has moved to Homewood Middle School. Our time is up at Shades Cahaba, and I hope it's not as long as before when I get to walk the hallways again.

Early in 2019, I realized Shades Cahaba would celebrate its 100th anniversary the next year, and I wanted to commemorate it. I have always been interested in oral histories and wished I had thought to collect family oral histories before my grandparents and older relatives had passed away. I put together a plan to gather oral histories from people who attend Shades Cahaba. Mainly those who went to high school, but the elementary school as well. I was hoping to collect them and share them with the library or whoever could keep digital records. Then I realized I should instead produce a podcast and share it with everyone. I had a plan.

I wasn't sure anyone at Shades Cahaba or the school board was celebrating this anniversary, so I contacted Principal John Lowry. He put me in touch with PTO President Alexa McElroy; they had a plan. They kicked off the school year with a celebration of the 100th year, and I happily volunteered my services.

The podcast was 23 episodes long and covered everything Shades Cahaba. From the high school to the elementary school and from the lunchroom to the underpass. I spoke with alumni, teachers, and principals who shared their stories of Shades Cahaba. I finished the podcast at the end of the school year in 2020.

There was so much I thought I knew about Shades Cahaba, but this podcast taught me so much more. I was able to find out if some fables I had heard over the years were true or not. And as a bonus, I was able to find out about the beginnings of the Homewood School System and the high school.

This project has been a labor of love to celebrate the school and the people who, let's face it, raised my children and me. And since I had collected so much information on the school, I decided to write a book to celebrate the 100th Anniversary of Shades Cahaba on September 19, 2020.

Shawn Wright
Homewood, Alabama 2020

CHAPTER ONE

Settlers in Shades Valley

RICH DEPOSITS OF IRON ORE, COAL AND LIMESTONE —
the three main ingredients used in making iron — are what brought the Elyton
Land Company to the beautiful Central Alabama, where they established the city
of Birmingham in 1871. The new city was nestled in what was known as Jones
Valley, the middle section of a 100-mile-long valley below the northern slope of
Red Mountain, which was mined heavily at the turn of the 20th century. Until the
deposits were exhausted, Red Mountain was dotted with mines, hoist houses, ore
crushers, and tipples. You could watch locomotives from the Birmingham Miner-
al Railroad steaming along the mountain's length, taking the ore to the furnaces
located close to the Warrior coal fields on the city's north side.

The other side of Red Mountain looked decidedly different, as it was heavily
forested with a creek running through the valley, which is known today as Shades
Valley. According to the tales of early 19th century traders, the local Indians called
the valley "Shades of Death" as the area was heavily populated with bears and wolves,
and many who entered the valley didn't return. To avoid trekking into the dangerous
valley, the Indians would travel along the tops of the adjacent mountains or cross the
valley only at established Indian trails. The rest they left to the wild animals.

The Creek Indian Nation controlled the area, however, their dominance was being threatened by American expansion from both the east and the west. When, in 1803, the United States purchased a huge amount of territory from France, known as the Louisiana Purchase, American expansion into Indian-controlled lands was in full swing. The Creek Nation was defeated in the Creek Indian War by American forces led by Andrew Jackson, and the area was opened up for home-steaders and investors. A few tribes remained in the area for several more decades, when the U.S. government forced their removal and marched the remaining Indians to Oklahoma in what would become known as "The Trail of Tears."

Homesteaders slowly trickled into the Shades Valley area. One of the first to settle in there was a soldier who had fought with Andrew Jackson in the Creek Indian War. Alabama officially became a state in 1819 and the legislature created Jefferson County soon thereafter, making land legally available for the first time.

Even as the city of Birmingham grew, what we now call the Over the Mountain area was still fairly untouched. Getting up and over the mountain was no easy task, and the length of the mountain made going around equally challenging. In the early 20th century, there were only a few gaps, or low areas in the mountain, where you could cross. These passages included Grace's Gap, Lone Pine Gap, Reader's Gap, and Brown's Gap.

Once roads were built and trolley service established, Shades Valley became more accessible. It was also desirable as the land was cheap and people wanted to escape the city's smog-filled downtown. The city's steel industry might have provided the financial engine that built Birmingham, but the blast mills and furnaces generated a tremendous amount of noise and smoke. Sloss Furnace was certainly one of the many culprits, as during this time, it was located right on the edge of the growing city. In fact, Nelson Real Estate Company, which developed the Hollywood neighborhood, even placed ads in the 1928 Shades Cahaba yearbook enticing home buyers with the slogan "Hollywood, Out of the Smoke Zone and into the Ozone."

A LOCAL EDUCATION

As more families moved into Shades Valley, the need for local schools become apparent as the trip over Red Mountain to schools located in and around Birmingham was too difficult. Some residents opened private schools such as Dalrymple Place in Edgewood where 25 students attended classes. The log-cabin school stood on Oxmoor Road where the Dawson Memorial Baptist Church parking deck is today.

The Rosedale community had schools for both black and white children. Black children attended Rosedale Public School, where respected community leader Sylvester Jones served as principal. White students attended Miss Kate Cumming school which she operated out of her home on Oxmoor Road. She described her school as a "select limited school for both sexes." Years before moving to Birmingham, Kate Cumming was a confederate civil war nurse who published her memoirs in 1866 under the title *A Journal of Hospital Life in the Confederate Army of Tennessee.*

Union Hill School was founded in 1867 to serve the children of the Waddell community, which was located where Mountain Brook Village is today. The school was sponsored by Union Hill Methodist Episcopal Church and housed in their building where Hollywood Boulevard crosses Highway 280 today.

ZELOSOPHIAN ACADEMY

Founded by Dr. James Hugh Blair Hall, the Zelosophian Academy opened in 1883 in the Oak Grove community with 96 students and five teachers. It was located on the corner of Oxmoor and Green Springs Highway in what we now call West Homewood. While a Shell gas station is there today, a plaque on a small concrete block on the corner of the property marks where the school once stood.

The school was associated with Oak Grove Cumberland Presbyterian Church

3

Dr. James Hugh Blair Hall in the upper left with his students.

and focused on primary preparatory and collegiate studies. It was known for music and art, as well as its emphasis on English studies and the history of Alabama. Hall advertised the Zelosophian Academy in The Alabama Cumberland Presbyterian newspaper as "the best school, with the best teachers and the best morals in the state." The school was featured in the book Where to educate, 1898-1899; a guide to the best private schools, higher institutions of learning, etc., in the United States by Grace Powers Thomas, which was published by Little, Brown and Company of Boston.

Hall's marketing efforts paid off and in addition to local children, many out-of-town students enrolled in the Academy. Most of these students boarded with families in the area, likely members of the Oak Grove Cumberland Presbyterian Church, when school was in session.

The Zelosophian Academy and Pleasant Hill Academy, located about twenty miles away in McCalla, were the only two schools in the area offering children a high school education, or what were called "senior level" classes back then. Pleasant Hill Academy was established by Isaac W. McAdory, who would go on to be the first Superintendent of the Jefferson County School system.

By the early 1900s, the Jefferson County School system was starting to build schools farther into the county. They opened Oak Grove School in 1908, just down the road from the Zelosophian Academy. It was a symbolic passing of the torch as Dr. James Hugh Blair Hall retired the same year.

1923 Domestic Science class

CHAPTER TWO

A New Consolidated
High School

IN 1907 A LAW WAS PASSED by the Alabama State Legislature to promote higher education in every county in the state. The "High School Law," as it was known, was created to give every boy and girl in the state the opportunity to take high school courses. The law required every county in the state to have at least one high school.

It would take until September 1916 for Jefferson County to open Boyles High School, now Tarrant High School. The school served all the white children who lived in Jefferson County which included those living in Shades Valley.

This is a good time to point out the law affected county schools and Boyles was the first Jefferson County high school. Birmingham already had its own school system which included Central High School, which was destroyed by a fire in 1918 and replaced by Phillips High School for white children, and Birmingham Industrial High School, later named Parker High School, for black children. If students from Shades Valley wanted to attend the closer Phillips High School, they had to pay tuition or travel to Boyles.

In an effort to increase the number of high schools in the state, the Alabama State Legislature passed a law in 1915 allowing for the creation of additional school districts within the counties. This allowed students the opportunity to attend a public school closer to their homes. Local citizens could vote to authorize a tax up to three mills to fund these area schools. This practice later became known as consolidation. The era of the one room school houses and schools in private homes was coming to an end as students were moving to new modern public schools.

STARTING A NEW SCHOOL

With the passing of the high school law, two Zelosophian Academy graduates, Will Franke and William Acton, both former students of Dr. James Hugh Blair Hall, started a campaign to convince the Jefferson County Board of Education to open a new school in Shades Valley. A special school district was created so tax funds could be raised for the school. They led a successful campaign and voters in this district approved a three-mill tax by a wide margin to fund construction a new high school.

This new school district was vast. It was 100 square miles and extended from the Birmingham city line south to the Cahaba River. It then stretched southwest to northeast, from the Shannon community to Argo and the St. Clair County line.

Ten acres were chosen at the junction formed by Montgomery Highway, Oxmoor Road, and Old Montevallo Road, what we now know as Hollywood Boulevard. Construction of the school started in 1919 and a three-wing brick building was built at the cost of $52,000. The school opened in 1920 with one principal, four high school grades, five teachers, and one hundred and fifty-six students.

Shades Cahaba was Jefferson County's first consolidated high school, but it wouldn't be the only one for long. By 1925, the number of high schools in Jefferson County increased from one to sixteen.

A NEW NAME

Students came from all over Shades Valley, and school officials invited everyone to help name the new school. They were given a ballot which read: "I suggest the following name for the new high school now being built in Shades Valley." The winning suggestion was Shades Cahaba High School. Unfortunately, the name of the person who submitted the winning name has been lost to time.

DEDICATING THE SCHOOL

Shades Cahaba was dedicated on Labor Day, September 6, 1920, a few weeks before the school opened it doors to students. The program called for addresses by Dr. N.R. Baker, Jefferson County Superintendent of Education, and Lieutenant-Governor Nathan Miller. Music was provided by the Alabama Boys' Industrial School Band and a dedication address by the University of Alabama Director of Extension, James S. Thomas. Memorial exercises were conducted by Miss Alma Rittenberry, a resident of Shades Valley.

The printed invitation to the event stated: "It is earnestly desired that every citizen of Shades Valley from Irondale to below Oxmoor and all up and down Shades Mountain and Cahaba river be present. This is our high school; a monument erected as a memorial to our solider boys from Shades-Cahaba in the World War. It is imperative that we open the school auspiciously. Come and bring a well-filled basket. It is very probable that Governor Kilby will deliver an address in the afternoon at the unveiling of the tablets. There will be games and music. Come and lend your presence. Show your interest and get acquainted with our county officials and faculty. Let's make this the best high school in the State." It was signed "Will F. Franke, Chairman; P.W. Acton and J.T. Tyler, Trustees; J.W. Ellenburg, Program Committee."

Later in the afternoon, after the formal addresses and a picnic dinner on the grounds, Mrs. Floribel Brown Ohme of the Board of Education, unveiled the "bronze tablets to the soldier boys of Shades-Cahaba." These are two large bronze plaques mounted on both sides of the auditorium doors, visible as soon as you walked into the new high school.

Both plaques say, "In honor of the boys and girls of this school district who served in the army or navy of the United States of America in the World War 1917-1919." The names of the individuals who served are split between the two plaques and those who lost their lives have a star by their names. At the bottom of the plaques, it says, "This tablet is dedicated by the residents of Shades Cahaba High School District 1-A 1919."

Dr. Baker said, "The Shades Cahaba building was built as a memorial to the memories of the names inscribed on the plaques." You can view the names in the Appendix of this book.

CHAPTER THREE

The School Opens
and the 1920s

SHADES CAHABA OPENED ITS DOORS to students on September 19, 1920. Students came from all parts of Shades Valley, such as Vestavia Hills, Cahaba Heights, Crestline, Irondale, Patton's Chapel, Edgewood, Grove Park, Oak Grove, Rosedale, and more. Children attended from surrounding farms as well. Elementary schools in the area became feeder schools for the new high school which included Crestline, Edgewood, Irondale, McElwain, New Merkle, Oxmoor, Patton's Chapel, Pleasant Valley, Rocky Ridge, Summit and Sulpher Springs.

Students traveled long distances to attend Shades Cahaba. To assist them, school officials provided transportation. Principal James Ward recalled, "early transportation consisted of open T-model trucks with roof and drop side curtains to keep out the cold and rain and plain boards up the sides for seats." One of the drivers of these trucks was O.A. Lindsey, better known to everyone as Uncle Ode.

Shades Cahaba was a modern school with all the newest conveniences, but there was no electricity until 1921. As I write this 100 years later, it sounds like

Shades Cahaba soon after it was built.

a huge inconvenience, as if things were not planned well enough. However, after conducting more research, I discovered only half of the homes in America had electricity in 1925. They had to wait a year, but it was still modern for its time.

THE SCHOOL IMPROVEMENT ASSOCIATION

Mr. Ward did a great deal for the school to get it off the ground and nurture it, but he couldn't have done anything without help from the Shades Cahaba School Improvement Association. This group of parents and interested adults was formed just a month after school started. By the second semester of 1922, just a little over a year later, the School Improvement Association had raised enough money to build a wood frame structure at the rear of the school. Half the space was used as the lunchroom, and the other half was the woodworking shop.

The State Department Division of Secondary Education judged the school was up to standards and was given it's accreditation. However, the Southern Association of Colleges and Secondary Institutions did not accredit the school. It seems the library only had 725 volumes, which the Southern Association deemed insufficient. Once the School Improvement Association found out, they sprung into action and helped increase the library's collection.

An article was even posted in *The Birmingham News* on January 24, 1921, titled "Pupils Want Books." It said, "there are 185 boys and girls who attend the Shades-Cahaba High School who are most anxious for a library." The article noted the students lived far from libraries and were soliciting for book donations. Principal Ward listed his address and phone number and encouraged all to donate books suitable to high school students. Through these efforts, the library was filled, and the Southern Association gave its endorsement.

Shades Cahaba's School Improvement Association soon became the P.T.A. (Parent Teacher Association) and is now the P.T.O. (Parent Teacher Organization).

UNION HILL SCHOOL

Shades Cahaba opened in 1920 as a high school, but elementary students moved in as well. The first elementary students came from Union Hill School, and they moved into a wooden two-room building just to the east of the Shades Cahaba Building. This building faced Hollywood Boulevard and was where the Homewood Chamber of Com-

Union Hill School

merce is now located, right above the current school playground. When Homewood started its own school system, the building was used as the Homewood Board of Education. The building had also been used as a band room and a Girl Scout hut, among other uses.

Union Hill School was part of Union Hill Methodist Episcopal church, and the school shared the same building as the congregation. The building was located right where the bridge is at Hollywood Boulevard and Highway 280. The highway was rerouted and widened in the 1950s, and any remaining buildings on the property would have been demolished during construction. Union Hill Cemetery, which still exists, shared the same property. The school was founded around 1867 by residents of the Waddell community, which was at Oxmoor and Cahaba Roads and is now known as Mountain Brook Village.

The Congregation of Union Hill Methodist Episcopal first merged with Mountain Brook Methodist in Crestline on October 10, 1948. And then merged with Canterbury United Methodist Church on October 12, 1952, becoming one of the largest churches in Mountain Brook today.

With the Shades Cahaba additions of 1927 and 1928 completed, grades three through six moved into the main building, and the first and second grades remained in the framed structure at the edge of the property. At this time, the elementary school and high school were placed under the same administration led by Principal James Ward. Grades seven through twelve were considered high school.

THE FIRST GRADUATING CLASS

There's a bit of controversy about who the first graduating class of Shades Cahaba High School actually was. I found this was true at Shades Valley High School and Homewood High School when those schools started. There's the first graduating class, the ones who graduated the first spring, and then there's the class who wants to assume the mantle of the first graduating class: the class who attended every year of the school. At Shades Cahaba, the class to claim the title is the class of 1923.

The first class to graduate was the class of 1921, and it consisted of four women: Jesse Ellezy, Lucile Watkins, Rexina Hubbard, and Inez Marable.

It seems the class of 1921 did not have a yearbook. It was likely not high on the priority list with trying to open a school and fill a library with books, but they still wanted to make their mark and leave their legacy. 1921 class historian Inez Marable was granted a page in the 1922 yearbook, and here is what she wrote.

"We, the first graduates of dear S.C.H.S. Oh! How proud we feel, and how dignified? Words cannot express our joy in filling the space in your annual with a few lines about us.

We have ample reason for being proud of Shades Cahaba, for it actually took us 6000 years to call her "ours," but nevertheless she stands as a monument in our lives which will fill our future years with gladness.

Now just a few personal facts about us. Our class consisted of four girls and a more happy bunch can never be found. What was our favorite study? Why geometry of course, just ask Miss Ellenburg.

Jesse Ellezy, must surely had our list, and as valedictorian for our class she certainly filled her place. She was always full of life and made sunshine wherever she went. As president of the Ward Society and also of the senior class. To her we owe much indeed. Lucile Watkins, (bachelor, we called her), and how did she derive her name? Why, she knew more old bachelors than we ever hope to meet, but a sweeter and smarter girl is hard to find.

Next Rexena Hubbard, it would take six thousand years more to make another like her. Rex, the sport of our class was never seen otherwise than neat, sweet and industrious all the time. Though she and the writer of this sketch had a little (???) trouble with Geometry, and we know Miss Ellenburg, was glad to get rid of us, nevertheless we'll try to make a success in something else.

This concludes the members of our class and our space is about filled, so to the class of 1922, we congratulate you, for you have some boys in your class, a privilege I assure you. And you didn't have to wait quite so long to graduate. Now we will say Farewell, Dear Shades-Cahaba, we will aye be true to thee."

~ Inez Marable, Class Historian 1921

HELEN COCKRELL

When Sue Grogan first became principal, she spoke at a P.T.O. meeting where she talked about the legacy of the school because "there are not many schools that have the kind of legacy that Shades Cahaba has in a community like Homewood."

Shades Cahaba High School alumni were actively participating in reunions during Grogan's time at the school. "I thought I was so fortunate to have landed there, and I had met some of the alumni that had attended when it was a high school, and the stories that they tell were just wonderful." Grogan was the person on staff who would open the doors, make sure the air conditioner was running, and take care of things for them. She always took the opportunity to sit down and talk to them about their memories of the school.

"One of the ladies was Helen Cockrell, who was well into her 90s, said that she attended the school the first year the school opened. She talked about what a wonderful opportunity it was to go to a school in the valley and that it opened the world to so many folks that otherwise would not have been able to attend." Helen showed Sue the trees the Arbor Society had planted around the school.

She told Grogan about riding her horse to school and where she would have to make sure the horse was tied up appropriately. Her baby brother had also attended school with her. "I ask about him," Grogan said, "and I think at the time he was 94. Her baby brother! Just wonderful, wonderful stories."

Helen Cockrell was very proud of being in the first class to attend all grades and graduate. "She talked about how wonderful that instruction was, but also how wonderful the opportunities were. She was on the women's basketball team," said

Helen Schnell Cockrell (second from right) and the 1923 girls basketball team.

Grogan. I mentioned I had a picture of the 1923 team but did not know who was who. "Well, she was a tall lady, and she talked with eyes sparkling about her time of being on that basketball team."

In one story from the book *Homewood: Life of a City*, Cockrell recalled the camaraderie, competition, and fun the girls had playing on a team together. She also enjoyed practicing with the boy's team, which was a necessity because gym space was scarce, and in the case of Shades Cahaba, nonexistent.

Over the years, it became more and more difficult for Cockrell to attend reunions, but Grogan would visit her at home and listen to her stories. "Another story that she told was about remembering hanging on a fence at the school, welcoming the troops. The boys, she said, who had gone to war. They were parading, marching down what is now Independence Drive as they were coming home, and how wonderful it was because so many of her friends that were students had gone to war."

Helen Cockrell passed away in 2013. She was 106 years old.

1927 Las Toreras Club

CHAPTER FOUR

The Lunchroom

THERE WAS NO LUNCHROOM when Shades Cahaba opened in 1920. Did the original planners assume students would bring their lunch, or did they think they could make it through the day without eating? The reason is lost to time, but it wasn't long before they realized they needed to feed their students.

The first semester, home economics teacher, Miss Blanche Evans, and a school maid would make sandwiches, soup, and milk for the students. The science lab was cleared during the lunch hours, and lunch was served between the beakers, vials, and bunsen burners. Serving lunch was a necessity and was not profitable. Instead of money, the school had to pay the maid in canned goods.

Sue Grogan enjoyed spending time with alumni during their reunions, and lunch was often a topic. The first principal was James Ward, and as a new principal herself, she asked them, "would you please tell me what it was that he did, that endeared you to him, and that you remember about him, and what he did to make this place a great place to come every day? Because I would like to be that kind of principal." And one gentleman said, "well, I don't remember much of what he did, but I do know that he came in our classroom every morning, early morning, and ask what we would like to have for lunch."

No one would deliver to Shades Cahaba because it was rural, and the mountain made it difficult to deliver supplies. The man told Grogan, "he took the truck and went into Birmingham and bought the food for that day and came back and gave it to the staff that was preparing the meal." Grogan continued, "and he said what a sacrifice that was for him every day. Now, I don't know that he would have done it every day and gotten his principal job done, but what a lovely memory that is."

Other people at the school probably did the shopping. Blanche Evans could have purchased groceries, but it would have been difficult for her to leave the school every day and continue to teach her students.

Author Sheryl Summe had heard the same gentleman who drove the school bus, which was a truck with benches and soft sides, would do some of the food runs. His name was O.A. Lindsay, and the students called him Uncle Ode. He was pretty adept at driving all-around Shades Valley, and he would have been an obvious choice.

Getting around Shades Valley today is nothing like what it was in the 1920s. The only way to get over the mountain was at the various natural gaps. The closest one to Homewood is Lone Pine Gap, where Vulcan is now located. It would have been difficult to access this gap in the early 1920s. It was called the Pig Trail due to the rough conditions of the road. Summe believes, "I really think most of the groceries and those kinds of supplies that came in and out of Homewood came on Oxmoor Road and then through what is today Mountain Brook and Montevallo Road."

The school improvement association made the lunchroom and library their top priorities, and by the second semester of 1922, raised enough money to build a wood frame structure at the rear of the school. Half the space was the lunchroom, the other a woodworking shop. This space was used until a new lunchroom could be constructed in 1927.

When the school expanded its eastern wing in 1927, a proper lunchroom was added to the basement, which was accessible via stairs inside and exterior doors on both sides. It was then the first full-time manager was hired—Mrs. Margie Cross who stayed for the next seven years.

Before we go any further, I feel we need to talk about Blanche Evans. She had earned her teaching certificate before coming to Shades Cahaba. After a few years, she went back to the University of Alabama, where she earned a degree in chemistry. She went to teach at Woodlawn High School and developed a hands-on approach to teaching her students about the natural world. Over the years, she became a conservationist and helped found various conservation organiza-

Blanche Evans

tions in Alabama. After retiring from teaching, she went on to become a nature writer. Blanche Evans Dean, as she was known, was inducted into the Alabama Women's Hall of Fame in 1985. A long way from making sandwiches in the science lab at Shades Cahaba High School.

IDA HAMLIN TYLER

As I interviewed people about Shades Cahaba, Ida Tyler's rolls kept coming up. Sixty-five years after she made her last rolls in the cafeteria, people could still smell them. I had to know more about Ida Tyler.

When Shades Cahaba's first lunchroom manager, Margie Cross, left the school in 1932, Principal Ward went in search of the next lunchroom manager. One of the applicants was Ida Tyler, a widower who was running a tea room on Highland Avenue in Birmingham at the time. The manager of the nearby Altamont/Claridge Manor apartments recommended her to Principal Ward. He said, "she is not only well versed in every department of a high-class grill or tearoom but is also a lady of very high character and personality."

The lunchroom in the 1940s

She accepted the job and started work during the height of the depression. Despite everything, the lunchroom went from debt to profit and from poorly equipped to well-equipped. She was a good manager and a great cook. Many considered her lunches to be the best in the country. One traveling salesman proclaimed they were "the best lunches between the Tennessee line and Florida line."

Ida had genuine Homewood connections and raised a family in Homewood who is here to this day. As I was researching her, I learned her great-grandson is Ken Kirk, a friend of mine since middle school. Ken and both of his sons are graduates of Homewood High School.

Her husband was Newton O. Tyler, a Methodist minister who was one of the first pastors at Trinity United Methodist Church in Homewood.

When Ida started work at the school, she probably had no idea she would stay as long as she did. She started work at Shades Cahaba in 1932 and worked until she retired in 1955. She died a few years later on June 23, 1957.

Herb Griffin, 1948 graduate, remembered her well. "We had good lunches, good lunches. It was run by a lady, Mrs. Tyler, an old lady. And she ran that thing like an iron ship. One of the mothers of a student also worked in the lunchroom serving the meals. It's just like it is today. You had a time of day for this class to eat, and the next class would come in the same way."

When I asked what his favorite meal was, he said. "I guess my favorite meal was on Friday. We started having fish on Friday because of all the Catholics. We had mashed potatoes and ground beef, I guess that was my favorite. And we had dessert which is standard in any school or any cafeteria."

Ida Tyler in the 1940s

Don Harbor entered the elementary school after Herb Griffin had graduated, and Mrs. Tyler was still at work. "The Lunchroom was in the basement at the rear of the school. You walked downstairs to reach it. There were windows facing the rear playground. I believe the walls were painted yellow. Mrs. Tyler was the head dietitian in the cafeteria. She was a large-boned woman with plain features and wire-rimmed glasses. She moved constantly with a purpose in mind though it often seemed she wasn't sure just what. She wore a white uniform and a hair net for health codes. In my early years the school lunch was 15¢. It included a plate lunch and a half pint of milk. Large oatmeal cookies were two for a penny. Sometimes I would bring my lunch from home but regularly my mother would give me the 15¢ and I would often buy two or four oatmeal cookies and a pint of milk for 3¢ and pocket the rest. The rest eventually wound up at the Homewood Hobby Shop."

1929 eighth grade class

CHAPTER FIVE

The 1930s

SHADES CAHABA OPENED ITS DOORS IN 1920 with five teachers, but by 1932 the school had twenty-two. The school had grown so much an associate-principal, J.W. Ellenburg, was hired to help with administrative duties.

Each day the students walked in the front door, and a statue of an owl would look down on them. The students and faculty embraced the owl, and it became more prominent throughout the school. The yearbook was called the "Owl," and the student newspaper was called "The Owlet" which was published as part of the Shades Valley Times newspaper.

The 1930s was when a couple of the school's longtime employees got their start. Lunchroom manager Ida Tyler started in 1932 and stayed until after the school became an Elementary School, retiring in 1955. And coach Piggy Mitchell was hired in 1934, leaving for the new Shades Valley High School in 1949.

The students at Shades Cahaba were very active in extracurricular activities and clubs. The school had an unusual number of literary societies, most of them dating back to when the school first opened. There were also other clubs such as the model airplane, hiking, and debate clubs. There was a place for everyone who attended Shades Cahaba.

The stock market had crashed on October 24, 1929, and the ensuing depression hit Birmingham hard. As Birmingham's economy worsened, so did Homewoods. And while they were two completely different cities, they shared the same county and Homewood's schools were county schools.

As the situation worsened, planned upgrades to the lunchroom at Shades Cahaba were canceled. By 1931, Jefferson County Schools cut teacher's salaries by 10 percent, and by Christmas, the teachers had only been paid for the first two months of the term. The 1931-1932 school year saw teachers paid with credit coupons for necessities such as groceries, gasoline, and oil. Even then, they were only paid for seven-and-a-half months of work instead of the usual nine.

By the spring of 1936, Jefferson County planned to close the school year early to save money. The city of Homewood made up the difference and was able to keep Shades Cahaba, Edgewood, and Rosedale schools open for the entire nine months of the school year. Homewood Mayor Bloom endorsed taking whatever actions were needed to keep the schools open and was willing to support whatever tax was required to do so. Citizens supported this even though they were going through hard times as well. Due to the community's sacrifice and support, Shades

Class from 1938

Cahaba High School was the only high school in Alabama to keep its Southern Association of Colleges and Secondary Schools accreditation throughout the depression. As horrible as the depression was, families with children had to face another silent enemy at the same time.

SOCIAL DISTANCING IN HOMEWOOD

In the spring of 2020, Shades Cahaba and other schools around the state shut down for in-class instruction due to the state of emergency declared by Alabama Governor Kay Ivey. Coronavirus, COVID-19, had been quickly spreading around the world and had made it to Homewood. To help slow the spread of the coronavirus, we were asked to participate in social distancing. We were asked to stay at home, not visit with other people, or gather in large crowds. It was thought if we avoid public spaces and limited our movement, the virus would be slowed, and our healthcare system would be able to handle the situation better. The school year was finished with children working from home and participating in video conferences. Our usual summer activities were put on hold.

This is not the first time Homewood and the rest of the nation have participated in social distancing. During the hot summer months of the 1930s and 1940s, infantile paralysis struck thousands of children each year nationwide. Three different, highly contagious polioviruses began with cold or flu-like symptoms and could permanently paralyze or kill infected children.

The disease hit its peak in the U.S. in 1952 and was at its worst in Jefferson County during the 1930s. It hit epidemic proportions in 1936. Parents did their version of social distancing by not letting their children play with others. The lucky ones would be left at rural camps such as Camp Winnataska for the summer, hoping they would be better protected at an isolated camp. But children are ingenious and have their own priorities. Author Sheryl Summe and I spoke about it.

"Thinking about the polio epidemics that came through Homewood is something I hadn't given a lot of thought to until I started interviewing people." Homewood did it's best to combat the disease. "Homewood actually had free spraying for kids. Kids would come in, and they would spray them with antiseptic. They were just trying to think of any way that they could forestall this. Parents that had their kids home from school wouldn't let their kids go out and play that whole summer because they were terrified."

One story Summe told stood out among many. "And this one lovely lady we interviewed, Anne Connolly Logan, lived on one side of Manhattan Street and her friend Emily Putnam lived on the other side of the street. And they would put notes in a lunchbox and throw it back and forth across the street. And then sometimes like a cookie or whatever. And that's the way they maintained their friendship that summer. And now I think about their parents being so terrified of this specter hanging over their children. And yet the children are more concerned with passing notes and cookies."

A KNOCK ON THE DOOR

Sue Grogan was working one Saturday afternoon at the school, trying to catch up on administrative work. She had been principal for two or three years and was the only one in the building. "I heard someone knocking on the front door. My office was kind of around the corner, so I didn't have a sightline to see who it was, and I thought it was probably some of the kids that were out playing soccer on the field, and they just wanted to come in and get a drink of water. So I get up from my desk and go to the door, and there is a middle-aged couple there. And when I answered the door and asked, May I help you? The gentleman said, 'Well, I know this is odd, but we saw a car out in front of the school. My mom is aging, and in her 90s, she attended Shades Cahaba High School. And shortly after she left Shades Cahaba in Birmingham, she moved to Atlanta and lived there for most of her life. But she asked that we take her on a memory tour of the Homewood area, and one of her requests was to come to Shades Cahaba. Is it okay if we just walk around the outside?'" Sue told him, "no, you must come in." For the next hour and a half, Sue gave a tour of the school to this former student, with all of her broken memories, and her son and daughter-in-law.

"Of course, the building had been changed, that had been added due to renovations. There were not many things that she remembered, but I thought, I'm going to take her to a few things and see if she remembers them. So we walked out to the court-yard where some stone steps were

At the original front door. The building in the background is where the Chevron station is now on Hollywood Boulevard and Independence Drive.

kind of in a circular pattern. And we went out there, and I said, Do you remember this area? It is now a garden for us. And we do some outside instruction here. But do you remember this? This might have been the way that you came out of school or came into the school." She didn't remember it.

They went to the auditorium. "And around the stage area are rosettes that go up on either side and across the top. I said, Do you remember this?" She said, "no, I don't." "We also have two plaques on either side of the auditorium doors in mem-ory of those Shades Cahaba District youth who fought in World War I. I asked her if she might remember those." She said, "no, she didn't."

Her son became a little disheartened his Mother was not remembering the school. Sue said, "I have one more thing that I want to show you." They went outside what would have been the front door for her, the doors facing Hollywood Boulevard. They went all the way down the sidewalk to the steps that go down to the horseshoe. They turned back to look at the building, and Sue pointed up. "If you look back upon the building, there is the owl, a three-foot concrete owl on top of the building. I said, might you remember that?" She brought her hands up to her face, and her eyes glowed. She said, "I do!" Then she said, "As a matter of fact. Go red, go black, push him back, push him back." Sue was surprised, "Were you a cheerleader?" And she said, "I sure was. And that was our cheer."

ELLENBURG FIELD

Today when you drive by Shades Cahaba School, you will notice a large field in the back. On school days, you may see entire grades of children running around the track and boys digging the dirt on the embankment next to Poinciana Drive. Things were different when this was a high school. This nondescript field is where Shades Cahaba High School battled it out with other area schools for athletic supremacy. It was known in the 1940s as Ellenburg Field, named after Shades Cahaba Professor J.W. Ellenburg,.

1945 Football team on east end of Ellenburg Field.

Majorettes on Ellenburg Field

During the 1936-37 school year, the football field was updated with the construction of permanent, concrete bleachers along the Poinciana Road side of the field. The same place boys today are digging in the dirt. The school provided funds for the materials and the W.P.A. (Works Projects Administration) provided the labor. There were also metal bleachers on the side of the field closest to the school. Neither of the sets of bleachers is there today.

The last remnants of the stadium were old goalposts at the ends of the field, leftovers from the glory days of Shades Cahaba Football. Those posts disappeared over time and were gone entirely by the late 1980s.

In 1939, the field received a considerable upgrade. Shades Cahaba became the only school in Alabama to have a lighted, all-sports field with speakers and an electronic scoreboard. A significant change considering only 19 years earlier when the school opened, it did not even have electricity in the school.

Jones Valley traveled to battle Shades Cahaba on Friday night, October 27, 1939. At halftime, a formal dedication of the new 48,000-watt lighted field was made by local dignitaries. Additional bleachers were added to accommodate the overflowing crowd who were expected to attend the game. More than 3,500 fans showed up to watch the game under the lights. Even with the additional seats provided by the Birmingham Baseball Club, spectators had to sit and stand around the field. Shades Cahaba thrilled the home crowd and won the game 33-6. They went undefeated in their remaining games, finishing with an 8-1 record for the season.

Herb Griffin had first-hand knowledge of the electronic scoreboard. "Well, they already had the field lights when I started there in the mid-40s. But the scoreboard, I know a little bit about scoreboard because since I couldn't play, I still wanted to work in athletics. So Piggy said 'Herb, you can run the scoreboard.'"

"The fellow that was in charge of the scoreboard was Byron Matthews; he was a year ahead of me." Then he explained, "The scoreboard was a wooden fixture, and it had bulbs screwed into the side of it, and on the end of the bulb, you had a switch you would click on. So if a runner ran 10 yards, you flick all ten of those bulbs."

The scoreboard was located on the east side of the field, farthest away from Montgomery Highway. It was at the end of the field just to the side of the goalpost. It wasn't there when I attended Shades Cahaba in the early 1970s. Herb said, "No, it was probably gone before I was finished. It didn't last long. But Alan Baker was on the sideline, they called it a sideline announcer, but he didn't announce. He had a telephone and would go up and down the sideline and call the scoreboard. Byron Matthews was called the play-by-play announcer, and Alan would call the information into Byron, and then Byron would call it out on the loudspeaker. 'Jones just ran for 10 yards...' That sort of thing." It seemed a little complicated. "It took three of us, only three of us. Byron was the main guy, there was Alan, and I flicked the lights."

CHAPTER SIX

The Building Grows

CONSTRUCTION ON THE ORIGINAL three-wing brick building began in 1919 at the cost of $52,000. When you entered the main entrance, which faced Hollywood Boulevard, there would be a hallway going left and right, which would take you to the two main halls with classrooms along the outside. Directly ahead of the front doors would be the auditorium. The auditorium was originally built with tall windows on both sides, which would let in natural light. Natural light would have been necessary since electricity would not have been run to the school until 1921. Large windows covered the length of one wall would open to let air circulate in the classrooms. Small potbelly stoves would be used to heat the classrooms during the coldest winter days.

In 1922, the School Improvement Association had raised enough money to construct an unfinished, unpainted, wood-frame building at the rear of the main building. It was built to serve as both a lunchroom and a wood shop. A temporary addition until something more permanent could be constructed.

The first addition was built in the summer of 1926 to help relieve overcrowding. This addition was on the Montgomery Highway side of the building (now Independence Drive). When I attended the school in the 1970s, I wondered about

If you look closely, you can see the opening in the arch along the
Montgomery Hghway side of the building

the series of steps in the middle of this long hallway. It consisted of a few short steps going down to a flat section, followed by more stairs going up. They were located where there is a large arch, visible on the side of the school. Today, it is a side entrance, but during my time at the school in the 1970s, it was a bathroom. This middle section of the hall never made sense to me.

When I talked with Sue Grogan about making lunches in the science lab, she said, "And, you know, there's an archway in the hallway that is closest to Highway 31. That was a pull-through driveway at one time, and I had been told that back in the day, that's where they would pull the food truck in after they had picked the food up."

Sure enough, if you look at a school photo from then, you can see the open space below the arch. Somewhere along the way, the entrance was closed, making one long hallway. Over time, the need for a pull-through went away, and the hall was enclosed from one end to the other, leaving random steps to confuse future elementary school students.

1926 was also the year Edgewood Elementary School opened. Elementary students were still attending Shades Cahaba, but those in Edgewood now had their own elementary school, which helped relieve overcrowding. 1926 was also when the communities of Edgewood, Rosedale, and Grove Park combined to create Homewood. The new city was starting to grow, and more room was needed for students.

A year later, in 1927, a second two-story addition was added to Shades Cahaba along the east side of the school. This addition included a new lunchroom in the basement, moving hungry students out of the wood-frame building behind the school.

When Shades Cahaba opened in 1920, students from Union Hill Methodist Episcopal School had moved into a wood frame building on school property facing Hollywood Boulevard. With the 1927 addition completed, the 3rd through 6th-grade elementary students were moved into the main building. The 1st and 2nd-grade students stayed in the small wooden structure where the current Homewood Chamber of Commerce building is today.

A third addition was constructed on the east side of the school and was called the grammar school wing. The 1st and 2nd-grade students were finally moved into the main building, bringing grades 1-12 together for the first time. This addition was paid for by the city of Homewood and completed in 1930.

A blueprint of the grammar school wing was found in the 1939 Jefferson County Board of Equalization appraisal files. It showed regular classrooms upstairs and science and biology labs, home economics, and boys and girls dressing rooms downstairs.

The communities to the west of Homewood were growing as well. In 1928 Hall-Kent Elementary school opened, replacing Oak Grove Elementary School,

The rear of the original school before construction of the two wings.

which had burned.

The depression of the 1930s took a toll on Shades Cahaba. The city and supporters worked hard just to keep the school open for a full 9-month session when most schools were closing after six months to save money. Money for repairs and maintenance was not readily available, and the school suffered because of it.

Wood frame building in 1939, located where the Homewood Chamber of Commerce is located.

In the 1940s, the school was completely repaired and repainted. A central heating system, radiators, and fluorescent lights were installed. By then, the student population topped over 1,000 students. Twice the students the elementary school has now. Even with the upgrades, it was apparent a new high school was needed. Shades Valley High School opened its doors in 1949, and Shades Cahaba became an elementary school.

Around 1952, Montgomery Highway was being widened due to growth south

The Grammar School wing in 1939. The gym would be built on this end a few decades later.

of Birmingham. Out of concern for student safety, a tunnel was created from Hill Food Store to the school. This tunnel became known as the underpass.

Not long after Shades Cahaba became an elementary school, Jefferson County and the City of Homewood provided funds to build a combination auditorium and gymnasium. This addition was built onto the end of what was known as the grammar school wing-back when it was a high school.

There would be no more construction on the school until the late 1980s when it became apparent Shades Cahaba needed more room. It would have been easier to build an entirely new school in many cases, but Shades Cahaba was spared. Before this new construction, there was a large courtyard between the two original wings and the extensions added in the 1920s. This area was filled with a new library, office, and lunchroom. The school's entrance was moved from the Hollywood Boulevard side of the school, the owl door, to the southwest corner of the school, which faces at an angle towards Independence Drive and the field. A new wing of classrooms was also added onto the east side of the gym built in the 1950s. This addition created two more stories of classrooms for the growing school.

CONSTRUCTION MEANS PROGRESS

If you attended Shades Cahaba or taught there during a construction project, you probably remember the inconveniences the projects brought with it. Kerney Ardillo taught for a couple of years at Shades Cahaba in the 1950s during a big construction project. The state widened Highway 31, right next to the school. There was no air conditioning in the school, and to stay cool, you had to keep the windows open. Her room was the first one on the corner facing Highway 31 and Hill's Grocery. They had to keep the windows open, and the dirt from the construction created a layer of dirt on everything. Parents would bring fans for the teachers to use in their battle against the dust and the heat.

Air conditioning would not come until the 1970s or later. In my memories, we did not have air conditioning in my classrooms in the early 1970s. The P.T.A.s fundraiser every year was selling Halloween candy. With some of the proceeds, they would have window air conditioning units installed. They were always being installed in the classrooms I was in the year before.

Kerney Ardillo's daughter, Laura Estes, better known as Ms. Matthews to her kindergarten classes, taught at Shades Cahaba as well. "When I first started Shades Cahaba, I was on the complete opposite end of the school, right above the parking lot. And the radiators. I would put the kids down for a nap every day around 12:30. And for some reason, that's when the pipes would start popping and banging. The only way we could control the heat in the room was to open and close the windows because it would be too hot or too cold. I was always opening and closing the windows."

The front of the school in 2020

A NEW LIBRARY AND MORE

Laura's mother taught at Shades Cahaba, but her father also had a connection to Shades Cahaba. "He was on the Homewood Board of Education for fifteen years and eventually was the President of the Board. He loved to be involved in all the construction and the reconstruction of the schools." She said, "He was very instrumental in making sure the buildings were what they needed to be for the children. And of course, I was there during the three million dollar renovation.

Well, for a full year, at least, you could walk down the hall, and there was Sheetrock dust everywhere. We were all getting sinus infections. And in fact, my doctor saw me so many times; he said to wear a mask." Of course, leave it to kids to find humor there. "So when I'd take the kids to lunch, I would put this mask on, and everybody was laughing at me. But it was wonderful when they got through with it. In fact, I got to be on the committee that told the board what kinds of things we wanted in the new building."

There were a few essential items to Laura and the other teachers. "Well, in kindergarten, we wanted a bathroom between the two classrooms, that was number one. And we didn't want concrete block walls, and we wanted Pella windows." The windows confused me, so Laura said, "Well, so that the blinds were in the middle of the two panes. Because during nap time, we wanted to pull those blinds down. Mr. Bumpus was the superintendent at the time and whatever we asked for we got. And I remember requesting that for kindergarten, we wanted tile in front of the sinks for our art tables." It only made sense. "Well, Tricia Simpson and I walked into the rooms as they were building them, and we saw they were going to carpet all the way over to the sink. And we called the board and said, no, no, no." Mr. Bumpus told the teachers to go in, chalk off where they wanted the tile, and they would get it.

The renovations at Shades Cahaba Elementary School in the late 1980s made the most significant impact on the school of any project up to that time. If you attended the school before then, you would have a hard time visualizing what the school looks like now.

If you attended Shades Cahaba after this renovation, you probably have a hard time visualizing what was there before. I always tell people the original part of the school was shaped like a big U with the auditorium at the bottom. If you were walking around the hallway, the inside of the U had windows looking out onto a big courtyard. And you could see the back and sides of the auditorium in this courtyard. During the renovation, the entire courtyard was filled with classrooms, a library, an office, and a cafeteria.

Laura said, "Well, my father and Mr. Bumpus were good buddies. And I think Mr. Bumpus had a vision, but my Dad kind of helped him follow through with all of it. I do remember that when it came time to buy the furniture for the new teacher's lounge after the renovation. My Dad said, 'get you a group together now. Go pick out something, and I will forfeit my salary,' I think it was three hundred a month to be on the board. And he said they could just take his money to get the furniture paid for." There was one stipulation. "He didn't want any smoking in the teacher's lounge. The original teacher's lounge was terrible."

CONSTRUCTION IN THE 21ST CENTURY

Shades Cahaba was well taken care of over the next couple of decades. Before the school centennial arrived in 2020, the lunchroom was updated, and security measures were added to the school. I'll let Principal John Lowry explain. "The school got a nice new cosmetic upgrade; I guess you could call it. New carpet, new wallpaper, and new paint in areas where we don't have wallpaper. The lunchroom has been updated with new flooring, new paint, new furniture, even a whole new layout in there. And that's the extent of the things that you can see. There's been a lot going on with some of the internal parts of the building. Our security cameras, the way the doors lock. The heating and cooling, the building management side of it. There's a whole new technology that comes with the upgrade that we didn't have, even ten years ago."

These are pretty significant upgrades for a 100-year-old building. Lowry continued, "And anybody that's done a home remodel here in Homewood knows that when you get into an old facility and start tearing out walls and doing things, sometimes you end up with a little more than you had planned on. And that's certainly been the case here. But this is a beautiful building, and it's got amazing bones. And it just held up well."

When I would talk to people about Shades Cahaba's history, one of the first questions would be, "are those beautiful wood floors still there?" And I would tell them, yes, but they are covered in carpet. And then they would ask, "but do they still squeak?" Yes, I would tell them, they still squeak. Everybody remembers the floors and the squeak.

Dr. Lowry said, "Yeah, the floors. They squeak even to the point that the way the lights in the building work is, they click on and off with sound. So if you're in a room and you're quiet and still for a few minutes, the light will turn off. And then when you move and make some noise, the lights will click on. But if you're here in the building early, before everyone else, and you walk down the hallway, the floors will squeak, and all the lights will come on at the same time because they can pick up the noise."

During the school's 100th anniversary, the school is poised to welcome Homewood students for many years.

The front door in 1948

CHAPTER SEVEN

The 1940s

THINGS WERE LOOKING UP for Shades Cahaba when the 1940s started. The school had the most modern athletics field in the county with lights, scoreboard, and permanent stands. The football and baseball teams were doing well under the guidance of Coach Piggy Mitchell. And the student population was continuing to grow and thrive under the leadership of Principal R.B. Nichols.

But in 1940, it was also apparent the United States would eventually become involved in the wars in Europe and Asia. Men from Homewood began volunteering for military service, which would become mandatory a year later.

Things would be different during the last decade of Shades Cahaba High School.

SCHOOL IMPROVEMENTS

Shades Cahaba was one of the most modern schools in Alabama when it opened in 1920. Additions made in 1926, 1928, and 1930 continued to improve the school. The depression made times tough for everyone in the 1930s, and not much was done to improve the school then. Just keeping the doors open was the primary goal. The country went to war in 1941 and many resources were directed towards the war effort. By 1944 there was no denying it; upgrades needed to be made at Shades Cahaba.

The Jefferson County Board of Education approved the much-needed improvements, and funds came from the Board of Education and Shades Cahaba's P.T.A. The P.T.A. had raised $10,000 for the updates, which included $2,500 donated by Birmingham industrialist and philanthropist Erskine Ramsey. If you are familiar with the name, Ramsey High School in the southside of Birmingham is named after him as well as bandleader and trumpeter Erksine Hawkins of "Tuxedo Junction" fame. Ramsey never married and had no children of his own, so he offered families a savings accounts at the Bank of Ensley with $100 for each child named after him. Hawkins's family took him up on the offer.

Plans were to install a central heating plant, modern lighting, and updated wiring throughout the school. Venetian blinds would be installed in all the classrooms to control the natural light and cut down on glare. Minor repairs and improvements would be made, and the whole building would be given a thorough cleaning.

Since the opening of the school, classrooms had been heated with individual pot-bellied stoves. The hallways and restrooms were not heated, which led to uncomfortable breaks between classes. The new heating system included a boiler house built on the end of the auditorium in the courtyard. This automatic, stoker-fired heating plant provided conditioned air for the entire school. This new system was radiators, and they would heat the school for decades to come.

A new modern lighting system of fluorescent lights was installed. A newspaper article said the new lights would provide "30

The pot bellied stoves would be replaced with radiators

units of lights compared with four units from the present system." A significant increase in the amount of lighting the students would have to work on their studies.

Most importantly, the school's wiring would be upgraded to handle the new lighting load, which would make the school safer. It couldn't have come sooner as the wiring may have already been condemned before the project started.

These projects did not go as smoothly as hoped. Updates to the school were halted due to a shortage of workers. Projects were happening all across the Jefferson County school system, not just at Shades Cahaba. Too many workers were serving in the military, and there was not enough manpower for all the projects to be completed quickly.

P.T.A. President Mrs. George Watson would not stand for the work stoppage. The P.T.A. did their part raising money for the upgrades, and she was concerned the condemned wiring system would start a fire. She had a point, many of the county's schools were new, due to the previous schools being destroyed by fire due to faulty wiring.

There was tension between Mrs. Watson and Principal Nichols over conditions at the school. Mrs. Watson said about the restrooms, "the toilet facilities for both high school and elementary grades are in a deplorable shape, even with the restroom doors closed, the odors in the hallways from these toilets are offensive!" Principal Nichols denied all the charges Watson threw his way.

Projects were eventually completed in time for the school to be heated before the cold of winter came. The improvements were nice, but the school was still crowded, and something needed to be done to fix the problem.

A CALL TO PARENTS

During World War II, people across our country made sacrifices by serving in both the military and our hometowns. Before the war, some people would maintain and make improvements at Shades Cahaba, but those people were off at war.

Parents helping construct a path in 1944

If there was going to be any maintenance at the school, the parents would have to do it.

A P.T.A. newsletter from 1944 summed it up well. "Remember way back before Pearl Harbor when Saturday afternoons meant putting on slacks and tennis shoes and sprawling in the hammock with a book; taking the wife and kids for a ride or just fishing? If there was any work to be done, George did it. But George is now far away doing other work, and it ain't trimming hedges brother like it used to be."

A call was put out to all parents and siblings old enough to work to come to the school and help clean up. There was general maintenance needed to be done and hedges to be trimmed. A walkway was also needed to be built.

There is an enclosed hallway connecting the grammar school wing to the main building with exterior doors across from each other in the middle of the hall. One set opens to the courtyard between lunchroom and grammar school addition. The other set of doors opens to the front of the school with a dirt, and sometimes muddy, path. A concrete path needed to be constructed to connect the door with the front of the school. Supplies would be provided, but parents were needed to build it. Parents and students dug out the path, constructed the forms, mixed and poured the concrete, and finished the path. They did an excellent job as this path exists to this day.

WORLD WAR II STUDENTS

Students from Shades Cahaba served bravely in the war and returned home, and some made the ultimate sacrifice. When the school was opened, it was dedicated to the memories of the "soldier boys of Shades-Cahaba." Another plaque was dedicated on Homecoming Day, October 24, 1946, to the boys who lost their lives in World War II. This ceremony included a gun salute, a prayer by an army chaplain, and a plaque presentation. The honored guests at the event were Mr. Aubrey Miller, former coach, and Mr. J. M. Ward, former principal. Names on the plaque are listed at the end of this book.

One of those names was W. Clem Mulkey, Captain of the 1936 Shades Cahaba Football Team. When the war started, he volunteered for the U.S. Army Air Corps. He died when his P-51 Mustang crashed when returning to England from a mission helping secure the beaches in France on D-Day.

In 1970, a new Alabama National Guard armory was built on the corner of Old Montgomery Highway and South Lakeshore Drive. It was named Fort William C. Mulkey in his honor in 1974.

TIME FOR A NEW SHADES CAHABA

In 1942, with the country fighting wars in Europe and the Pacific, Homewood could no longer ignore it, Shades Cahaba was getting a little old in the tooth, and it would have to be replaced in the next decade.

The Homewood City Council began addressing the problem with Council-man Lewis Williams reporting, "For the past five years there has been something like a net gain of five hundred new families in Homewood and most of them have from three to five children of school age."

The council decided to meet with the Jefferson County Board of Education and let them know the needs of the schools in Homewood were not being met. A report was completed by the spring of 1943.

Homewood was willing to help finance the construction of a new high school, but Superintendent Dr. John E. Bryan felt the idea was ridiculous. Their study had shown the enlargement and improvement plans for Jefferson County schools were adequate. You see, Shades Cahaba and other schools had been built so they could be expanded, and county officials just wanted to add one more wing onto the old building.

When the student population at Shades Cahaba topped 1,000 in the mid-for-ties, area citizens demanded the finest high school and would accept nothing less. By comparison, Shades Cahaba currently has a student population in the low 500s, and there is more room now than the school had in the 1940s.

When the citizens demanded such an excellent high school, Dr. Bryan coun-tered, "a champagne school could not be built on a beer pocketbook."

In his defense, the school system was not in a position to start building every-where there was crowding going on. The war was still raging and would not end until September 1945, and resources were needed there.

There was talk about Homewood and the newly incorporated Mountain Brook getting together with the county to build the school. In January 1945, the mayors of the two cities applied to the Bureau of Educational Research at the University of Alabama to begin a feasibility study. The study was favorable to the idea.

Committees were put together to explore the possibility of a special election to finance the cities' part and educate the public on the need for a new school and why they should pass it. A headline in the *Shades Valley Sun* on April 20, 1945, read, "Recommend new $500,000 high school for Shades Valley." The wheels were beginning to turn, and two years later, the cities voted in favor of a five-mill tax. Some of the funds were to be used for their part of the new school.

I have always been impressed with Homewood residents stepping up to support the school's needs, even before Homewood became Homewood. In this case, the public was a little unenthusiastic about it. Turnout was very low, and the tax passed with 278 votes for and 125 votes against.

The Jefferson County Board of Education purchased some swampland in the Sweetwater Park Survey, which was outside the Birmingham city limits. If you are not familiar with the property, it would have been to the east of the Rosedale neighborhood. This part of town would disappear a little over a decade later due to the Red Mountain Expressway construction. It is directly north of Hermosa Drive and the beginning of Poinciana Drive in Hollywood. The school was on the other side of Highway 280, and the BB&T Bank Building is on the corner of the property, and the Mountain Brook YMCA is at the back of the property. It is also next to the Birmingham Zoo, which would not be built until 1955, a few years after the high school opened.

The school project was started with a winning bid of $2,100,000. Much higher than the $500,000 cost floated by the *Shades Valley Sun* and Homewood leaders a few years before.

Frank Peake, formerly principal of Hewitt-Trussville High School, was appointed principal of the new school. He worked out of Homewood City Hall until the school was built. Horton Chamblee and Ouida Hightower, teachers and counselors at Shades Cahaba, became counselors at the new school, and Coach Piggy Mitchell continued as the football coach.

Everything is great! There is a new, modern school, plenty of room for growth, everyone's happy, right? Wrong.

The board of education decided to leave the name Shades Cahaba with the elementary school, and they chose Shades Valley as the name of the new high

Shades Valley High School

school. They did take the Mountaineers' mascot and red and black colors to the new school.

A letter signed by more than 1,600 students and graduates protested the name change. The Homewood City Council, Shades Valley Exchange Club, and Shades Valley Athletic Association presented resolutions to the board requesting the name be kept Shades Cahaba High School. None of it worked.

Shades Cahaba graduated their last class around June 1, 1949, and on September 7-9, the remaining high school students registered for Shades Valley High School at the Homewood City Hall. Shades Valley opened its doors to 870 students and 44 teachers on September 12, 1949.

The new students were ready for classes in the fall of 1949, but the school wasn't quite ready. Only the west wing was completed when classes started. It contained the offices, library, and just ten classrooms. Classroom space needed to be found, so the library housed seven classes, and two other classes met on school buses. Other students sat in chairs and desks in the hallways. The band and graphic art department continued to use the facilities at Shades Cahaba, and Ellenburg Field at Shades Cahaba hosted one more year of athletic competitions.

There was also no parking or landscaping at Shades Valley. Teachers and students had to park in the surrounding neighborhoods and walk through muddy fields and construction debris to get to class.

The rest of the school was completed during the first school year, and the auditorium was the last piece. It was completed just in time for graduation in 1950.

The school was built to ease overcrowding at Shades Cahaba and to be a much more modern facility. Despite this, the post-war baby boom was higher than the planning allowed. Initial enrollment was 870 in the fall of 1949. It was 1,456 in 1955 and 1,701 in 1956. Within six short years, the student population had doubled in size and had outgrown the facility. The school had initially been built for 1,500 students.

Shades Valley High School was expected to be, and was, "the showplace of the south." The curriculum emphasized college prep. The school had successful athletics teams, student organizations, and the college board recognized it as one of the outstanding secondary schools in the nation.

Shades Valley was initially designed to serve students from across Homewood, Mountain Brook, Vestavia Hills, and Hoover. To relieve overcrowding, Berry High School opened in 1959 for Vestavia and Hoover students. Eventually, both of these cities created their school systems. Mountain Brook created its school system in 1966, and Homewood created its school system in 1970.

At this point, Shades Valley was landlocked in Homewood, and it served students who lived elsewhere who had to drive across town to the school. In 1996, Shades Valley relocated to Old Leeds Road in the Irondale Community, and the original school was demolished.

Shades Cahaba outlived the building built to replace it.

1945 cheerleading team

CHAPTER EIGHT

Athletics at Shades Cahaba

AS SOON AS THE SCHOOL WAS BUILT and the doors opened to students, teams were formed, and athletes began preparations to compete against other Birmingham area high schools.

According to the Owl yearbook, the first football team did not start practice until a year later on September 30, 1921. Shades Cahaba's first game was on October 7, 1921, with an unfortunate loss to Bessemer 56-0. The first win came the next week over Inter-Church 7-6 and then Jones Valley 35-0 the following week. There was a loss to Simpson then a win at Woodlawn, and the team ended the season with a loss to Jefferson County 39-0. Not a bad start for a first-year football team.

According to the Alabama High School Football Historical Society website, the first Shades Cahaba football team featured fullback Guy Acton who earned first-team all-state player recognition.

The Owl yearbook gave an overview of the season and ended with this paragraph: "Much interest was shown in football by the entire student body. Most of us were green about football, but learned that it was a very exciting as well as interesting game."

Football was here to stay at Shades Cahaba.

FOOTBALL COACHES

Coaches at Shades Cahaba generally coached all the teams the school fielded, football, baseball, and sometimes basketball. Most of them taught classes or served in the school administration as well. Longevity seemed to be an issue as the first four years, brought four different coaches.

ARTHUR ACTON

Acton coached in 1921 and had a 3-3 football record and left after one year.

W.A. REEVES

Reeves coached in 1922 and had a 0-4-1 football record, leaving after one year.

SUMPTER CLARK

Clarke, better known as Sump, coached in 1923 and had a 6-2-1 football record during his only season.

Coach Clarke showed up to meet his team two weeks after fall practice had started. Mr. McInnis, better known as Coach Mack, had been running practices

Arthur Acton

W.A. Reeves

until he could get there. He greeted the team, had a hard workout, and then picked his starters for the upcoming games. It must have worked because Shades Cahaba went on to have their first winning record.

Sump Clarke coached Shades Cahaba in the middle of his professional baseball career. He played minor league ball starting in 1918 for Baltimore and Brantford in Canada. He played with the Birmingham Barons in 1922 and 1923 and was called up to the Cleveland Indians at the end of the season. and explains why he was late for football in the fall.

Clarke may have returned to Birmingham to become Shades Cahaba's coach, but there was another reason he returned. He married Agnes Pauline Ash of Birmingham on February 8, 1924. He left the school with his wife in tow to play for the Cleveland Indians in 1924. Clarke continued to play and manage in the minors, making stops at Albany, New Orleans, and Atlanta before finishing his career at Springfield in 1933.

AUBREY MILLER

Stability came with Coach Aubrey Miller, who stayed for three seasons, 1924-1926, and compiled a 10-7-5 football record. He was so well-thought-of by the

Sumpter Clarke   *Aubrey Miller*

students they dedicated the 1927 yearbook to him knowing he was leaving at the end of the school year. He left for Greenville High School, where he coached until 1935 when he resigned to take the job as principal of Repton High School in Conecuh County, Alabama. Coach Miller returned to Shades Cahaba in 1946 as an honored guest when the school dedicated a plaque to "the boys who lost their lives in World War II."

SIDNEY MALLOY

In 1927 Sidney Malloy, a Birmingham-Southern College graduate, came to Shades Cahaba to coach football, baseball and teach history. His football team's record was 1-15-1. His first year saw defeats by 59-0, 71-0, and 87-0. There are no records of the baseball team's scores, but it must not have been much better as Coach Malloy left after two years. His next stop was Pensacola High School.

ROBERT R. HARDY

Next came Robert R. Hardy, who was the coach and athletic director for the 1929-1933 seasons and had a 21-16-6 football record. Hardy graduated from Elon College and was also the history teacher at Shades Cahaba. Shades Cahaba

Sidney Malloy   *Robert R. Hardy*

yearbooks called him "Hammerhead" Hardy. There was no mention if it was from his playing days or his coaching style.

The first decade at Shades Cahaba saw six different coaches field teams. R.R. Hardy was coach at the beginning of the 1930s, and he gave way to Shades Cahaba's final coach, Piggy Mitchell.

PIGGY MITCHELL

Oren Prentice Mitchell, better known as Piggy Mitchell, coached at Shades Cahaba from 1934-1949 and was also a teacher and assistant principal.

He was born in 1900 in Bibb County, Alabama, and graduated from Simpson High School in Birmingham in 1919. He went on to get his degree from Valparaiso University in Indiana.

His first head coaching job came in 1928 at Bankhead High School in Cordova, where he stayed for three seasons. He then coached at Valley Head from 1931-33 before taking over at Shades Cahaba in 1934 and coaching for the next seventeen seasons. His football teams combined for a 100-47-6 record, and all but two of them finished with winning records, and five squads finished with only one loss.

He moved to the newly opened Shades Valley High School for the 1950 season before moving to Hewitt-Trussville High School in 1951. Following the 1963 season, Mitchell retired from the football field with a of 180-120-20 over 37 seasons as a head coach.

Coach Mitchell made a significant impression on the students and athletes he coached and taught over the years.

Oren P. "Piggy" Mitchell

Herb Griffin has some great memories of Piggy Mitchell, not just from Shades Cahaba but also from the YMCA and the community where he coached and served.

"Piggy Mitchell worked on the playground in summer. He worked with boy's baseball, also football, but mostly baseball. He knew everything you wanted to know about baseball. Anyway, we had a 17-year-old basketball team that was second to none. I think we played one ballgame, and coach Mitchell saw that we were superior to any team in the league. I had nothing to do with it. I was just a substitute on the team. He knew nothing about basketball. Nothing! We laughed about it often. He took that team, and we played in 1948 and 1949 and went undefeated."

Coach Mitchell was ahead of his time in many aspects of high school athletics. He brought basketball to the county schools without gyms by starting a dirt court league, where you guessed it, they played on dirt courts. He introduced wrestling to the county schools, and he brought the T-formation offense to high school football teams in Birmingham.

As Herb Griffin mentioned, he loved baseball. Mitchell was the founder of the Jefferson County baseball league and was its president from 1935-1965. He organized the city leagues, making it so schools could play each other in tournaments, and he organized the East-West ball game. As Shades Cahaba baseball coach, he led teams to three Jefferson County Championships.

Shades Cahaba would play baseball games at Rickwood Field, and Herb Griffin made it a point to attend all the games, even if the school was in session. "So, you had to really try hard to get in trouble at Shades Cahaba," Herb said. "Shades Cahaba always had a good baseball team, and they would play games at Rickwood Field, so I thought I was supposed to go to all of them. I didn't go to school when we had ballgames at Rickwood." He never got in trouble because he had a friend in the administration. "You know how I would get back? I would hitch a ride with Mr. Nichols. He'd never turn me in. He'd bring me home every time and never ask me what I was doing out of school."

Years after leaving Shades Cahaba, Herb told me he had the privilege to serve on one special committee. "Coach Mitchell's family had contacted Fletcher Allen, he was probably the best-known athlete at Shades Cahaba, and they said 'we want to get dad in the Hall of Fame.' Fletcher talked to the Alabama Sports Hall of Fame but would get no help from them whatsoever. They were not interested in high school athletics. They were interested in college, professional, and so forth. So we started working with the Alabama High School Athletic Association in Montgomery, they were trying to set up a Hall of Fame."

Coach Mitchell served as president of the AHSAA Fifth District Board for 25 years. He was inducted into the Alabama High School Athletic Associations Hall of Fame in 1996.

BASKETBALL

Basketball got its start at Shades Cahaba in 1921. Unlike the other sports, it seems the school may have struggled a bit as the Owl yearbook stated: "they did not show up as well as other teams, and they were scheduled against some of the

The first boys basketball team in 1922

The first girls basketball team in 1922

strongest teams in the state."

1921 was also the first year of the Alabama State High School Athletic Association's statewide basketball tournament in Birmingham. The eventual state winner was Central of Birmingham, one of Shades Cahaba's opponents.

Girls Basketball also got its start in 1922 with Miss Mary Spencer as the coach. The 1922 yearbook described them this way: "The team was composed of hard fighters, and a good team was the result of their efforts. Much pep was manifested by them as well as good work."

One of those players was Helen Cockrell, who loved the opportunity to play on the basketball team. Sue Grogan told me, "Well, she was a tall lady, and she talked with eyes sparkling about her time being on the basketball team!" She loved the camaraderie with her teammates and the opportunity to practice with the boy's team because gym space was scarce.

It seems basketball for boys and girls left the school not long after it started, and the 1928 yearbook makes no mention of the sport. The 1932 Owl yearbook mentions a boys team and they won only one game against superior teams.

The 1927 baseball team

BASEBALL

The 1922 yearbook, says, "The Shades-Cahaba High School baseball team is the outstanding sport, it seems as if everyone knows about baseball than other sport, and our boys are just naturally good players." One of the players was Guy Acton, our all-state fullback from the football team. He pitched and played center field.

During Coach Mitchell's time as the baseball coach, Shades Cahaba's teams went to ten of fourteen county playoffs and winning three county championships. Baseball was his favorite sport, after all.

Unfortunately, there is not a lot of information on the Shades Cahaba baseball team's records. In many cases, yearbooks would have a team photo or maybe a roster, but the yearbook would have been sent to press before the baseball teams completed the season.

Believe it or not, there was even a Girls Baseball team. In 1923, the Shades Cahaba Girls Baseball team was the county champions. Why? Because there were only two teams, the other team was Fairfield. During the first game, Shades Cahaba won at home 7-4. In the second game, Shades Cahaba ventured to Fairfield and beat them there, 6-4. The principal, Mr. Ward, was the coach.

One of the pitchers on the team was Bess Fortenberry. In 1932 she would purchase a hot dog and sandwich "stand" and rename it the Irondale Cafe. She and her cafe would be immortalized in the book "Fried Green Tomatoes at the Whistle Stop Cafe," written by her niece Fannie Flagg. The story was loosely based on Bess and her whistle stop cafe and was made into a movie called "Fried Green Tomatoes" in 1991.

ARMISTICE DAY FOOTBALL GAME

1947 was a banner year for the Coach Mitchell led football team. Shades Cahaba was invited to play powerhouse Aliceville in the 1947 Armistice Day Game at Legion Field. The hype was overwhelming as Shades Cahaba and Aliceville were both undefeated going into the game. There was a mammoth parade in downtown Birmingham preceding the game, and General Omar Bradley gave a speech at halftime. Birmingham News reporter Joe Justice wrote, "This looks like the big one, so the Mounties aren't likely to be in a losing mood! With Aliceville of the same mind, how can the general fail to get his money's worth?" Unfortunately, this was not Shades Cahaba's day as Aliceville won 18-6, the only loss suffered by the team. Even still, the Mounties went on to be the county champions.

This day was a little more special than you might think. Armistice Day was created to celebrate veterans of World War I. Shades Cahaba was also built as a memorial to these same soldiers. Veteran and Birmingham resident Raymond

Weeks led an effort to change Armistice Day from one recognizing just World War I veterans to one recognizing all veterans. His efforts paid off when a bill to recognize the day, Veterans Day, as a national holiday, was signed by President Eisenhower on June 1, 1954.

The parade before the Shades Cahaba - Aliceville game was the first Veterans Day parade held in Birmingham. A tradition lasting to this day and is one of the largest in the nation.

The 1947 football team

Principal James Ward in 1938

CHAPTER NINE

Principals at Shades Cahaba

THERE WERE JUST NINE PRINCIPALS at Shades Cahaba School during its first 100 years. The first principal was James Ward, who stayed in the role for 23 years, making him the longest-serving of all the principals. Ward and R.B. Nichols were the only two principals of the high school, the rest serving as elementary school principals.

JAMES WARD, 1920-1943

James Ward received his undergraduate degree from Alabama and his master's degree at Columbia before coming to Shades Cahaba. Ward was a bachelor when he first became principal, but he wouldn't stay single for long. Before the beginning of the second school year, Ward married Miss Narvia Faucette on September 7, 1921. After a brief honeymoon, Mrs. Ward joined her husband at Shades Cahaba, where she taught domestic science and arts according to a wedding notice in the September 11, 1921 edition of *The Birmingham News*.

After a long and distinguished career at Shades Cahaba, the Jefferson County Board of Education moved Ward from his principal position and assigned him the supervisor's job in the attendance department in 1943. While the position seemed like a promotion and included an increase in salary, it appears Ward was strong-armed into taking the position. Area residents were not happy, and a petition from approximately 1,500 citizens was presented to the board by Will Franke, spokesman for the group. They wanted their principal back. Unfortunately, county politics prevailed, and James Ward's tenure as Principal of Shades Cahaba High School was over.

ROBERT B. NICHOLS, 1943-1951

When James Ward moved to the board of education, Robert Nichols, better known as R.B. Nichols, became principal. Nichols was Principal when the high school students moved to the newly opened Shades Valley High School, and he stayed to run Shades Cahaba Elementary School.

Nichols was Don Harbor's first principal, and he remembers him well. "The school principal though my Third Grade year was Robert B. Nichols, a tall, heavyset middle-aged man with a ruddy complexion and kinky white hair. We rarely saw him with his coat on. He wore thick glasses and wore suspenders supporting baggy pants, which gave him an almost slapdash appearance. He seemed to be perpetually happy, smiling all the time. He loved children, and I remember him reading stories to us from time to time."

When I asked Herb Griffin if his Principal stood out, he replied: "Yeah. God, we loved the Principal! His name was R. B. Nichols. He was about six-foot-eight or six-foot-nine. Giant of a man! He had hands twice as big as mine; each hand would be bigger than both of my hands put together. He was a giant of a man!"

Before the 1951-52 school year, R.B. Nichols became principal at Bluff Park School on Shades Mountain. He swapped jobs with Lelton B. Cobb, who had been Principal at Bluff Park for two years.

LELTON B. COBB, 1951-1963

Lelton Cobb taught in the Walker County School System from 1934 to 1949 before moving to Bluff Park School as Principal.

"Lelton Cobb became principal when I entered the fourth grade and remained so for my remaining years," said Don Harbor. "He was tall and slim with a prominent nose that gave him an air of authority. He had a slightly dark complexion with well barbered slicked back black hair that gave him a somewhat exotic appearance. He dressed as would a successful businessman and projected an air of formal authority. The polar opposite of the disheveled Mr. Nichols. Yet he was kind, patient, and sensitive to the expanding issues of growing children. And, much appreciated, he never really put much force into a paddle stroke."

After serving 12 years as Principal, Cobb was appointed Principal at Leeds High School by the Jefferson County Board of Education.

MARGARET VINES, 1963-1970

Margaret Vines came to Shades Cahaba from Pinson Junior High School in 1963. She was very active in professional associations and had previously served as president of the Alabama Education Association (A.E.A.) and chairman of the Jefferson County Elementary Principals Association. She received her under-

graduate degree from Birmingham-Southern College and masters from the University of Alabama. When Homewood started it's own school system, teachers and administrators were given the choice to joining the new school system or remain with the Jefferson County School system. Vines chose to stay with Jefferson County and she moved to Rocky Ridge Elementary School where she served as Principal until 1976.

LOUIS LEVAUGHN, 1970–1981

Louis LeVaughn came to the Shades Cahaba after spending 14 years as Principal of Green Acres Elementary School. At Shades Cahaba, LeVaughn was a champion of mainstreaming special-education students who craved inclusion in the school. He made sure these students were not socially isolated, as was the habit of most schools. When hearing one of his students wanted to have books to take home, just like the other students, he made sure they had some. LeVaughn also oversaw the return of the owl to the school in 1978.

On a personal note, Mr. LeVaughn was my Principal when I attended Shades Cahaba. I enjoyed having Mr. LeVaughn as my Principal, and only later in life did I find out he had served in the Marine Corps in World War II. He was a fire control radar operator from 1943-46 in the Pacific theatre with the 7th Anti-Aircraft Artillery Defense Battalion. He was awarded a Battle Star for action on Angaur in the Palau Islands of the Western Pacific. In September 1945, he took part in the ceremony of the Japanese surrender in Tsingtao, China.

MIKE MILLER, 1981-1989

Mike Miller served as Principal from 1981–1989. He had been the Assistant Principal and choir director at Homewood High School before coming to Shades Cahaba.

KAREN DELANO, 1989-2000

Karen DeLano came to Shades Cahaba from the Elmore County Public School System, where she served as a curriculum coordinator. She would serve as principal for just over a decade before leaving to be an assistant school superintendent in Vestavia Hills. She finished her career as superintendent of the Auburn City Schools in 2019.

SUE GROGAN, 2000–2013

Sue Grogan came to Shades Cahaba in 1988. She was initially a guidance counselor and served in the role for six years, moving from part-time to full time after a year. Grogan moved to an administrative role with the title of instruction support, which later became the Assistant Principal position. When the Principal job opened, she threw her name in the hat and

was named Principal of Shades Cahaba. She served as Principal for 13 years until her retirement, a total of 25 years at Shades Cahaba.

JOHN LOWRY, 2013–PRESENT

John Lowry came to Shades Cahaba from Creek View Elementary, where he served as assistant principal for four years. He served as an Assistant Vice Principal with Sue Grogan and became Principal when Grogan retired in 2013. Lowry was the Principal during Shades Cahaba's 100th year. Even though he did not attend Shades Cahaba as a student, he has a strong connection. His wife attended Shades Cahaba.

CHAPTER TEN

The Shades Cahaba Owl

WHEN YOU STEP INTO THE FRONT LOBBY at Shades Cahaba Elementary School today, you are greeted by a large owl which has been expertly crafted in commercial linoleum in the middle of the floor. On the walls of the lobby are large colorful owl illustrations framed in shadow boxes. When you walk the hallways, you will start to notice the owls on classroom doors, on the decorations in the hallways and on the shirts of the children you pass. You will see fliers for events such as the "Owl Prowl," a race starting at the school before taking a short lap through the streets of Hollywood and finishing where it began. If you are a first time visitor to Shades Cahaba Elementary, it would be hard not to realize the owl is the school mascot.

But why the owl? There are many other options like Eagles, Bulldogs, Tigers, Lions, Wildcats; the list goes on and on. What about the Patriots, the mascot Homewood High School Students chose for the new high school in 1972?

When the school opened in 1920 until the high school students left for Shades Valley, high above the original front door stood a 900 lb., 3-foot tall concrete owl, watching over the students as they entered the school. This owl was not the athletic team mascot; there was no Shades Cahaba Owls; instead, it was called "a symbol of learning to all who enter here."

While not the mascot, the owl was still a big part of the school. The yearbook was called "The Owl," and an early student newspaper was called the "Owlette." During the forties, a group of Shades Cahaba High School students called themselves the "Owl's Club,"and organized dances for fellow students at City Hall.

The athletic teams chose a mascot much different than an owl. They were called the "Mountaineers" or "Mounties" for short. There is a photo of Coach Piggy Mitchell wearing a shirt with Shades Cahaba written on the top, Mountaineers on the bottom, and has an owl image in the middle. Most would find this confusing, but for those of us in Alabama, we are used to seeing this. Our largest universities have a combination of mascots and slogans which don't have anything to do with each other. Auburn University uses Tigers and Eagles, and the University of Alabama is called the Crimson Tide and has Elephants. Shades Cahaba had an Owl and a Mountie.

I attended Shades Cahaba in the early '70s, and I had no idea the owl had

ever existed. There were no owl images in the hallway or on the floor. We didn't have an Owl yearbook or Owlette newspaper. There was no talk of the owl because there was no owl on top of the school.

So, where did the owl go? Before we answer, we need to look back on the last days of Shades Cahaba as a high school.

During the 1940s, Shades Cahaba High School was

grossly overcrowded with population well about 1,000 students. There were students in grades 1-12 in less space than there is now, which has houses grades K-5. I have a hard time imagining so many people in such a small school.

Since the 1940s, Shades Cahaba has added a considerable amount of space for students. In the 1950s, the school added a gym and later, classrooms were added to the east side of the gym. In the late 1980s, construction elimi-nated the courtyard and added a library, office, lunchroom, and extra classrooms in its place. By comparison, today's elementary student population is in the low 500s. Half what it was in the 1940s.

Student hijinx

By 1944, citizens of Homewood mobilized to push for a new high school in Shades Valley. And I don't mean to ruin the surprise, but they got one built. The Class of 1949 was the last high school graduating class at Shades Cahaba before the high school grades moved to the new school.

Homewood citizens and officials pushed to keep the name Shades Cahaba, but county officials refused, and the name Shades Valley was chosen. The new school mascot continued to be the Mountaineers, and the red and black team colors are still used to this day.

When the last graduating class left Shades Cahaba, so did the owl.

As I was researching this book, I found different tales about what happened to the owl. One was the owl was removed from Shades Cahaba so it could be transferred to the new Shades Valley High School, but they didn't want it. While Shades Cahaba had the owl to welcome you to the building, Shades Valley had a Tower with a clock on the front. The yearbook was even called the "Tower."

Another rumor was there were student hijinks involved. The class of 1948 had a 30th reunion, and they had published a newsletter called "The Mountaineer." In a story about the owl, it was written, "It seems that Teenie Boppers of the late 40s would splatter a fresh coat of paint on the owl every Halloween and the officials had the owl removed."

Some people believe the owl was stolen, but I had a hard time imagining the removal of a 900 lb. concrete owl from the roof without damaging the roof or the owl. No matter the rumor, the owl was removed from the roof and forgotten.

During my middle school years, I was hanging out with friends when one of them wanted to show us something. We headed down Wellington Road and entered an overgrown area between two homes. There in the middle was this huge owl on a short pedestal. It was then I learned about the owl at Shades Cahaba.

A few years later, in 1978, the owl was returned to its perch on top of Shades Cahaba Elementary School, and the explosion of owl pictures and decorations descended on the school.

When I created the Shades Cahaba Oral History Project, the owl's story was the first story I wanted to learn about. I started asking around, and everyone had a different story. A lot of time has passed since the owl was put back on the roof and even more since it was removed. Memories have started to fade, and people who were part of the story are no longer with us.

I decided to set the record straight, and all it was going to take was talk to a few people who might know the story. This is going to be easy, right? I asked author Sheryl Summe who wrote the book *Homewood: The Life of a City*, how I would go about finding information.

She said, "Well, you go back to the newspaper or whatever published source there was from the time as the definitive source. They thought that the owl came down when it was going to be moved to be put on Shades Valley High School, which seemed to be right. But then it sort of, somehow, got lost. Whether anybody stole it or not, who knows? You would never know. But you can start with the definitive source and then add those stories on the side."

Someone recommended I talk to former kindergarten teacher Laura Estes. It seems Laura lived next door to the owl, could it be her fathers, former Homewood Board of Education president Nick Ardillo? Would she know the story?

When I asked her if she knew anything about the owl, she said, "Well, my dad built the house that we lived in on Wellington Road. And Mr. Farris lived next door, an older man. I think what I heard was he found out that the owl was in storage at the maintenance department, and he got it, and had a platform built with cement and put the owl on there. And then he had a little circular garden around it. Real pretty, but then lots and lots of trees. And so you had to know it was there, to know it was there. Well, I was 12 when we moved there, and I would get a book and a blanket and sit under the owl and read. It was wonderful."

Someone else suggested I reach out to Dale Turnbough. You see, Dale is the step-daughter of Louis LeVaughn, who was principal when the owl was returned to the school's roof. Maybe she would know?

Dale had been a staff writer at the *Birmingham Post-Herald* back in the '70s. Just my luck, she had written an article on the history of the owl. She gave me an approximate date it would have been published, and after a short search on microfilm at the Linn-Henley Research Library, I found it.

For you kids who might be reading this, microfilm is where you have to go when the internet fails you. You will have a greater love for the search feature on your computer, where on microfilm, you have to look at Every. Single. Page. On Every. Single. Day. Just to find the article you want.

Dale's article coincided with the 57th-anniversary celebration which was held at Shades Cahaba. It seems the owl had just been "found." Of course, some of us already knew about it.

According to Larry Farris, whose grandfather James M. Farris, was once the superintendent of the Jefferson County Board of Education, the owl came down because "they were tired of having to clean the owl every year by Halloween pranksters. I guess the thing had 15 or 20 gallons of paint dumped on it."

Larry's grandfather saw it in storage, and he asked the board what they were going to do with it. They didn't have any plans, and he either bought it from the board, or the board gifted it to him. He took it to his home on Wellington Road, cleaned it up and put it in his garden on the side of his house where it stayed.

After Larry's grandfather died, he sold the house and lot to Ed Landmon, a Shades Cahaba alumnus. And then Larry sold the owl for $75 to Bert Lindbergh in October 1976.

The owl had been "found" and the anniversary committee had high hopes for getting the owl back on the roof of the school in time for the cel-

The owl being returned in 1978

ebration, but Mr. Lindbergh had other ideas. "I don't blame them for wanting it back, but I've got it, and I want to keep it. I still intend to move it to my home, and I am not interested in parting with it." Lindbergh said the owl is a "one of a kind thing. No one does that sort of artwork anymore." Mr. Lindbergh had plans to take the owl to his home on Shades Mountain and place it on a pedestal overlooking the valley below.

That would seem like the end of the story until the class of 1948 got involved. The next year was the 30th Anniversary of their graduation, and they had plans for the owl. I will let class president Herb Griffin tell it from here.

"I remember how we got the owl back. We had a Shades Cahaba Class of 1948 reunion committee, and one of the influential members of that committee was Jesse Todd. And supposedly Jesse and several other influential members of the committee went to see the man who had the owl and suggested very strongly that he present it to the school. They convinced him that he needed to do it even though he purchased the owl legitimately. It was his owl; nobody doubted that. They suggested it would be in his favor if he returned the owl to the school, and he did."

There was a lot of excitement about the owl going back up on the roof of Shades Cahaba. Homewood Board of Education Superintendent Bill Cleveland was a student, and he remembered it well.

"I remember it was a big deal. We all went out to what was the front of the school. I remember us all going out to that area, and the crane hoisting up the owl. We had a big ceremony about the owl returning. It was pretty memorable."

After my podcast episode about the owl had been published, I received an email from Shades Valley High School alumnus Don Roberts. He grew up in Edgewood, and his mother graduated from Shades Cahaba around 1935. Don wrote, "The owl was in storage at Shades Valley High School in the backstage area of the auditorium when I was a student there from 1961-64. I remember it being spattered with various colors of paint."

Now we have an answer to a lingering question. Was the owl removed with the expectation it would be used and displayed at Shades Valley High School? Yes, it was, and no, they didn't want to display it. The paint suggests the story about pranksters painting the owl is correct as well.

The owl has been back for a long time and will continue to watch over the school and be a symbol of learning to all who enter there.

Patricia Simpson's class in the 1990s

CHAPTER ELEVEN

Elementary Schools in Homewood

EVEN THOUGH THIS BOOK is about Shades Cahaba, there are other elementary schools in the Homewood area deserving of mention. In an earlier chapter, we talked about how residents established schools to educate youth in Shades Valley. With more and more people moving to the valley, more schools were needed to serve a growing population. These schools eventually gave way to more modern schools established by the Jefferson County Board of Education.

EDGEWOOD ELEMENTARY

The community of Edgewood became a full-fledge town in 1920, and soon after, leaders decided they needed their own school. Six acres of land just off Broadway was purchased, and the town deeded five of the acres to the Jefferson County Board of Education in 1924. Before the school was even completed, the School Improvement Association, which would later become the Parent Teacher Association (P.T.A.), started identifying and supplying the schools needs. One of the

Edgewood Elementary School in 1959

first needs was a road. Edgewood School was built on a "muddy field" without a road leading to it. The School Improvement Association petitioned the town for a road. They got their wish, and a gravel road from Oxmoor Road was soon opened. A path on the north side of the school was created as well and went from east to west. This path did not access Oxmoor or Broadway but was eventually extended, turned into a road, and renamed College Avenue.

Edgewood Elementary was completed in April 1926 and opened in September with 100 students and four teachers. The school had Grades 1-8, and the only way they could function with only four teachers was to have two grades for each teacher. First and second together, third and fourth, fifth and sixth and seventh and eighth.

Just like Shades Cahaba, Edgewood had the same pressing needs, a substantial library collection and a need to serve lunch were only two of them. During the first couple of years, students brought their lunch. By 1928 an inexpensive room was built on the back of the building to serve as a lunchroom.

The first addition to the school was completed in 1930, which added four more classrooms and a lunchroom in the basement.

The Homewood Civic Club organized a band in 1932 and Kindergarten in 1934. Edgewood Elementary continued to grow over the years.

On a Friday evening, November 13, 1953, Mrs. E.H. Todd noticed flames coming from the rear of the school's east wing. A fire had started in the basement lunchroom—firefighters from Homewood, Mountain Brook, and Birmingham came to help. By the time the fire was extinguished, the lunchroom and ten classrooms were utterly destroyed, and two other classrooms were damaged.

The school could be rebuilt, but the immediate need was what to do with the students. Roughly half of the 900 students would need a place to be educated. Offers came from all over, and authorities settled on a proposal from the Birmingham City Schools to use the vacant Paul Hayne Vocational School building. The school was located on 20th Street South in Birmingham's southside. The Kirkland Clinic is located on the block the school was located in. Six, seventh and eighth graders were bused to the Paul Hayne school building while the rest of the school stayed in the undamaged part of Edgewood Elementary.

Edgewood continues to operate in the same building, and many additions later is Homewood's largest elementary school.

HALL-KENT ELEMENTARY

Oak Grove, which we now know as West Homewood, was annexed into the city of Homewood in 1955. The annexation brought Hall-Kent Elementary into the Homewood Family of schools. Schools in this area go back to the 19th century and include the Zelosophian Academy, which is essential to the story of Shades Cahaba High School.

Hall-Kent originally began as Oak Grove Elementary School in 1908 at the corner of Oxmoor and Greensprings. In 1927 Oak Grove Elementary School burned to the ground, and before Jefferson County could rebuild, some of the teachers started teaching in the Odd Fellows Hall, which was at the junction of

Two views of Hall-Kent Elementary School in 1959

Oxmoor Road, Oak Grove Road, and Gillon Drive. This location would have been about where The Briary pipe shop is located across the street from Pizzeria GM.

If you have never heard of the Odd Fellows, it is a fraternal lodge similar to the Freemasons, a fraternal lodge going back to the 18th Century in England.

Oak Grove landowner and dairyman Raleigh Kent, Sr. and his wife, Edna Mae, donated four lots in the neighborhood, and county school officials purchased the fifth lot and rebuilt where the school stands now. The school was completed in 1928 and had outdoor plumbing and water.

The school was named in honor of the Kent family and Dr. James Hugh Blair Hall, who was the founder of the Zelosophian Academy and established its roots in the community.

Children came from the communities of Oak Grove, Green Springs, and Shades Mountain. Once bus service was established, additional students came from Spaulding, Shannon, and Oxmoor to the west.

One notable achievement at Hall-Kent was they had the first kindergarten program in the state of Alabama established in the early 1930s. The P.T.A. was instrumental in promoting and gaining public support for kindergarten classes statewide.

All the Homewood elementary schools host carnival fundraisers. Shades Cahaba hosts a Winter Festival, and Edgewood hosts a Spring Festival. Hall-Kent hosted it's first Fall Festival years before the others. The first one was in 1935, specifically to help raise money to buy lunchroom equipment.

Over the next few decades, the school grew rapidly due to the number of students moving into the area. The post-war baby boom also had a considerable impact on the school.

A fire severely damaged Edgewood school, and Hall-Kent was built because Oak Grove Elementary was destroyed by fire. In April 1965, you guessed it; a fire broke out at Hall-Kent. The school's wooden portion was destroyed, which included the library, several classrooms, the boiler room, and the lunchroom.

This fire did not affect the students the way the Edgewood fire did. While the lunchroom was being repaired, part of the office was converted to a "sack lunch preparation center." It was challenging to prepare a balanced lunch, but P.T.A. volunteer Mrs. John Moses joked, "As long as we have peanut butter, the children will think they are well fed."

The three elementary schools in Homewood all started in the 1920s, Shades Cahaba, Edgewood, and Hall-Kent. There is one more we need to remember, Rosedale School.

Rosedale School in 1959

ROSEDALE SCHOOL

Community leader and educator B.M. Montgomery established a school for black children in the 1920s in Rosedale Park and initially met in Montgomery's home. Sometimes in the 1930s, the students moved to a wooden building built on the hill in the northeastern section of the community. The school was damaged by fire twice under suspicious circumstances.

The wooden school building was replaced in 1944 with a new building made of native rocks and masonry. It was constructed by the Works Progress Administration and built on four acres of property donated by local businessman Damon Lee, Sr.

Rosedale School initially taught elementary school students. The administrators and teachers made an effort to teach advanced grades and foreign language in the curriculum. Due to the communities efforts, Rosedale School was the first Jefferson County school for black children, and one of the first in the state, to teach classes above the junior high level. What's remarkable is they were able to do this during the heights of the depression. The quality of the education was such that when Jefferson County schools integrated in 1967, they were able to join the formerly whites-only schools without missing a beat.

When the schools integrated, Rosedale School closed its doors, but not for the last time. The building became the campus of Shades Valley Resource Learning Center, better known as R.L.C. When the new Shades Valley High School was completed in Irondale, R.L.C. moved there to the new campus. In 1996 the former R.L.C. building was purchased by the Birmingham Islamic Society and is home to the Islamic Academy of Alabama.

Rosedale School was an excellent school, and over 1,100 students graduated from 1937 to 1968. Some of their alumni are names you know or should know. Here are just a few.

Isaiah Robinson, Jr. — Tuskegee Airman and the first African-American President of the New York City Board of Education.

Fred Shuttlesworth — Civil rights activist, founder of the Southern Christian Leadership Conference and pastor. I could write a whole book on him alone, and some people have. Let's just say he was so important to Birmingham, the city renamed the airport in his honor.

Shelley Stewart — Former radio personality and advertising executive. He became the majority owner of a Birmingham ad agency now known as 02 Ideas.

Dr. Mamie Foster — a longtime educator and most important to our story about schools in Homewood, was a member of the first Homewood Board of Education and helped set the school system on a path we are on today.

I can't leave Rosedale School without mentioning their athletic teams, which had the greatest nickname in athletics, The Sons of Kong. What a great name!

FIRES

What is unique about these three schools is each one has experienced a devastating fire.

On Friday evening, November 13, 1953, Mrs. E.H. Todd noticed flames coming from the rear of the east wing of Edgewood Elementary School. A fire had started in the basement lunchroom. Firefighters from Homewood, Mountain Brook, and Birmingham convened at the school. Still, by the time the fire was extinguished, the lunchroom and ten classrooms were destroyed, with two other classrooms suffering damage.

Until repairs could be made, sixth, seventh, and eighth-graders were bused to the vacant Paul Hayne Vocational School building on Birmingham's southside. The rest of the school was able to stay in the whole part of Edgewood Elementary.

We already know Oak Grove School was destroyed by fire, but Hall-Kent Elementary School also suffered a fire in April 1965 when a wooden portion of the school was damaged. The library, several classrooms, the boiler room, and the lunchroom were all damaged.

The fire did not affect the students the way the Edgewood fire did. While the lunchroom was being repaired, part of the office was converted to a "sack lunch preparation center." It was challenging to prepare a balanced lunch, but P.T.A. volunteer Mrs. John Moses joked, "As long as we have peanut butter, the children will think they are well fed."

Two suspicious fires also damaged Rosedale School during its history. When the school was rebuilt the final time, it was made of native rocks and masonry to replace the wooden structure. The building was built on four acres of property donated by local businessman Damon Lee, Sr. And constructed by the W.P.A. (Works Progress Administration) opening in 1944.

CHAPTER TWELVE

Don Harbor's School Days

DON HARBOR WORKED WITH MY FATHER at Luckie & Forney Advertising here in Birmingham after he graduated college. Don moved on to a successful career in advertising, including a stop in Virginia. He eventually moved back to Birmingham and transitioned to a career as a commercial photographer, which is where I met Don. I have enjoyed working with Don professionally, but I most enjoy sitting around and listening to his stories.

I remembered he attended Shades Cahaba, so when I started the Shades Cahaba Oral History Project, he was the first person I spoke with. We had a great conversation, and he shared with me his memories of Shades Cahaba he had written some years before. He has allowed me to share them with you.

SECOND GRADE 1949-1950

My Second Grade teacher was Mrs. Lurlie Franke. She was tall, matronly, slightly heavyset with jet black hair that was very long. She wore it in a bun on top of her head. She still drove a Model A Ford that looked very old to me in 1949, though it was less than twenty years old at that time. I remember her as very patient and kind.

I believe this was the year of the "Dick and Jane" books though I may have read them the previous year. I do remember that there was an experimental group selected to learn Spanish. There was an area sort of roped off on one side of the classroom next to some bookshelves that were under windows. The selected students sat there during the lessons. I still have my Spanish-English dictionary, though I have no memory of Spanish.

One day at lunch in the second grade, Mrs. Tyler was not amused and continually grabbed the salt shaker away from me. After a few days of this, she sent me to the Principal's office. Mr. Nichols gave me a stern talk, but I could tell he was suppressing laughter. I must have stopped, but I remember trying it again at home from time to time for several years. Feels good!

I remember one day in the lunchroom accidentally sitting on a piece of roast beef and it became mired in the cord of my brown corduroy knickers. I found this icky, and it upset me to have to scrape it away. This turned me against roast beef for a while.

I have two outdoor memories from this year that the high school was still there.

One was a May Day celebration when they had us young kids dance around a Maypole while wearing crowns made from flowers. It was staged in the front playground just behind the Girl Scout building. The May Pole was one of the play sets, a tall metal post with about a dozen chains hanging with grip handles on the ends. I was so embarrassed.

The other was a ceremony of some type held in the football field. It may have been the same May Day event. I remember being mightily impressed by the marching band blasting and pounding their way past where I was standing. I had never seen anything like that. The next year the band was gone to the new high school.

Miss Manor's third grade class. Don is on the first row, third from the left

THIRD GRADE 1950-1951

My Third Grade teacher was Miss Barbara Manor. Miss Manor was a tall, strikingly handsome woman with long jet black hair worn in either a ponytail or in a bun on the back of her head. Unlike the other teachers, Miss Manor dressed in stylish, though conservative, clothing. She walked very erect like a fashion model and did interesting things with her hands as she talked. She reeked of elegance. I was madly in love with her.

One of the biggest events of my life up to this point was the purchase of my first pair of blue jeans and of Keds tennis shoes. Up until this year, I had worn green and brown corduroy knickers and some sort of clunky brown shoes. I hated these pants and shoes with a passion. I have never owned anything made with corduroy since.

Around 1950, Day-Glo colors began to appear on various consumer items. My mother bought me a pair of Day-Glo green and orange socks. I was so proud of them! I would have her stand on the front porch and watch me as I walked up the hill to-wards the school. "Can you still see me?" I would yell as I progressed until out of sight.

I had three pretend girlfriends that year: Janet McAllister, Nancy Harned, and Nancy Ann McNutt.

Janet McAllister lived near me on Hollywood Boulevard, and we would sometimes walk home from school together. She was a beautiful brunette and very friendly. I sometimes carried her books all the way to her house, then turned around to walk a block back to my own home.

Nancy Harned lived on Roxbury Road, just two houses south of the old Homewood Library on Oxmoor Road. She was tall with a prominent nose that gave her a distinctive profile that captured my little heart. I often dreamed about Nancy.

Nancy Ann McNutt lived in the last house on Poinciana Drive before the entrance to Lane Park and Shades Valley High School, just a block from my house. She was a tiny girl with freckles and reddish hair she wore in two long pigtails. She sat in front of me part of the year and was very talkative.

Our desks had an ink well in the upper right-hand corner. We would dip a quill pen into the India ink and practice writing cursive script sentences. One day I dipped one of Nancy Ann's ponytails into the ink. Neither she nor Miss Manor was amused, but I think Mr. Nichols in the Principal's office had trouble stifling laughter. The second time I did it, he was no longer amused.

Shortly before the end of the school year, we had a class photo taken with us, all sitting on some steps in the rear of the school. I still have an 8"x10" print with the names of each student printed with pencil on the back. Other than the yearly school portraits, this is the only photo evidence I have of my school years.

FOURTH AND FIFTH GRADE 1951-1953

My Fourth Grade teacher was Mrs. Lois Harper. Mrs. Harper was a small mousy woman of average build of the type who slither through grocery stores wearing dowdy dresses. She had curly salt and pepper hair and wore glasses. She seemed to have a constant smirking smile as her beady eyes peered over her glasses. She paced the floor a lot.

I only remember one event from that year. It was one that altered my course for nearly two decades, in a most negative way.

Up to this point, I had an active interest in girls, and always had at least one pretend girlfriend. I had no inhibitions dealing with them and often did so in both the classroom and on the playground. Evidently, too much so for Mrs. Harper's liking. One of my girlfriends sat right in front of me, and I often talked to her when I shouldn't have. Tired of warning me, Mrs. Harper sent me to the Principal's office at least once. Undeterred, I continued talking.

So one day, Mrs. Harper decided to cure me once and for all. And she did.

As I remember, it was mid-morning when she caught me talking. She made me get up and sit next to the girl at her desk for the rest of the day. The seat was so narrow we were pressed together. Of course, the whole class giggled the rest of the day. I remember Mrs. Harper smirking with contentment from time to time.

It worked. I became frightened of girls and unable to deal with them until I was an adult. Not that I had no desire. I was just scared to make that first gesture. Thanks to Mrs. Harper.

My Fifth Grade teacher was Mrs. Miriam Snuggs. She was a tall, lean, severe woman who rarely smiled. She had a homely face with piercing blue eyes behind steel-rimmed glasses. Her hair was a reddish dark blond worn in a tight, braided bun. She dressed in neutral color suits with white blouses as would an office worker. The combination was very imposing, though lacking personality. I remember her as soft-spoken, very kind, and patient. I liked her very much, but I remember nothing else about that year.

OTHER TEACHERS

The physical education teacher was a blustery man named Mr. Murphy. We called him "Old Man Erpy." He was a stout, large man, physically fit, with faded red hair and a red complexion from much exposure to the sun. In warm weather, he dressed as if on a safari complete with a pith helmet. It made him look funny to children, but I suppose it made sense to someone who spent the day outdoors, given the primitive clothing technology of the day. Boys often teased him unmercifully, and he would sometimes become flustered by it, but he was a patient man and mainly took it in his stride.

P.E. instructors Carol Scott and J.E.Murphy

There were two playgrounds, one in front of the school featuring swings and playground equipment, and a combination baseball/football field in the rear. It seems like we played in the front playground in the lower grades and switched to the rear field in the upper grades.

When I was in the seventh grade, the new gym building was opened, and much of our physical education classes were moved to there, particularly in bad weather. It was set up as a basketball court though other activities were held there. Other than the following incident, I don't remember any other specifics about it.

Mrs. Rice was the music teacher. I believe she traveled between several schools, and we only saw her once a week or so. There was an upright piano in the classroom, and she would lead us in simple songs. Gilbert and Sullivan songs were favorites of hers. Little Buttercup, etc. She was a large-boned middle-aged woman with graying hair. She wore steel-rimmed glasses that accented her homely face. But, oh, did she take all so very seriously! She loved her job, and her enthusiasm was contagious. I'm sure she was responsible for laying a foundation for my later love of music. Dear, dear Mrs. Rice.

Mrs. Frances Robinson was the school librarian. She had been at the school since it opened in 1920 and had taught English most of those years. She was small and frail with a pale complexion and pure white hair accented by thick steel-rimmed glasses. She mainly sat at her desk in the front of the room and rarely said a word unless there was a disturbance of some sort. I remember one day, all the kids in the room dropped their books on the floor at the same time when a signal was given by the instigator. Might have been me, I don't remember. I did such things and was no stranger to the Principal's office.

Throughout my tenure at Shades Cahaba, there were two teachers in each grade level up through Grade Eight. They usually faced each other across the hallway. I believe that each successive year, they would try to mix students from different teachers so that everyone will eventually share classroom time together. In the lower grades, I remember boys on the playground bragging that their teacher was better than mine. The First Grade was at the rear of the left-wing. Each grade progressed forward until Grade Six became the first classrooms encountered upon entering the hallway. Grades Seven and Eight were in the right-wing. Though I believe my Fourth Grade classroom was at the rear of the right-wing. I remember the windows facing the rear playground rather than the Montgomery Highway.

~ Don Harbor

Mrs. Florence Allen's class in 1963

CHAPTER THIRTEEN

The 1950s and 1960s

SHADES CAHABA SOLELY BECAME an elementary school in the fall of 1949. The high school students left to attend the new Shades Valley High School, but R.B. Nichols stayed at Shades Cahaba to continue serving as principal. Unfortunately, the owl took flight and would not be seen again for the next 28 years.

In 1947, Homewood citizens went to the polls and voted for a five-mill tax to help build Shades Valley High School. Not all of the tax went to Shades Valley, part of it went to build a Junior High School in Homewood. The doors opened at Homewood Junior High in 1957, and even more students left Shades Cahaba. Grades 7-9 would be attending the new school, leaving grades 1-6 behind. This move happened at Edgewood and Hall-Kent as well. Within a decade, Shades Cahaba went from having over 1,000 students roaming the hallways to less than half.

Another shakeup came in 1954 when Lelton Cobb was appointed principal of the school. Cobb was just the third principal in the first 34 years of the school's existence.

MONTGOMERY HIGHWAY

If you can believe it, Montgomery Highway, also known as and Highway 31 and most recently Independence Drive, was a sleepy country road. Over the years, the city grew, and the towns south of Homewood grew, creating more traffic on Montgomery Highway.

Traveling from downtown Birmingham to Vestavia Hills today is very simple. You would take the Elton B. Stephens Expressway, which locals call Red Mountain Expressway, which turns into Independence Drive in Homewood. You would pass by Shades Cahaba, crest the hill at Saulter Road and venture down the hill to Shades Creek before climbing the mountain to Vestavia Hills. If you could catch the green lights, this trip would take mere minutes.

Before 1970, this trip was much different. The typical way you would travel from Birmingham would start at Lone Pine Gap by Vulcan. The highway would continue into downtown Homewood, around the curve, past City Hall, and eventually Shades Cahaba. At Salter Road, the highway would wind it's way to Shades Creek and then up the mountain to Vestavia Hills.

Improvements started on Montgomery Highway in the 1940s, including adding the straighter and steeper four-lane road up Shades Mountain that we are now familiar with. The road would travel past what would become Brookwood Hospital a few decades later. At the bottom of the hill, a bridge was constructed at Shades Creek Parkway and a larger road built to Salter Road and Old Montgomery Highway.

Construction lasted into the '50s, and this entire roadway was widened and improved. Alumnus Don Harbor mentioned that the boys in his class loved to play in the bushes and undergrowth that separated Shades Cahaba and Montgomery Highway, only to be removed during road construction. Harbor said, "When I was first there, Highway 31 was just a two-lane road, and along it were shrubs and trees that were deep. We built a tunnel through the shrubs, and we would play games in there. And I can remember being very disappointed when they added the four lanes to Highway 31, and they tore all of that away, and there was only a fence left."

THE UNDERPASS

More roads meant more traffic, so a "student underpass" was added to link the western access of Oxmoor Road with Shades Cahaba School. But it didn't go as smoothly as you might expect. On March 16, 1952, *The Birmingham News* reported: "The fur was still flying Saturday over the proposed widening of the

Montgomery Highway from Bob's Tourist Court to Oxmoor Road in Homewood."

It seems there was a dispute over the right of way, and Hill's Grocery had some concerns about the underpass. Without getting into the nitty-gritty of the issues, let's just say Hill's Grocery was going to lose quite a bit of parking and was hoping to get the project eliminated. And, they were upset the highway project was encroaching on their property. You

Exiting the Underpass

may be thinking, where is Hill's Grocery? It is now the Piggly Wiggly.

Over the next couple of months, issues were worked out, and the only thing left to be decided was to have stairs or ramp access. The ramp won, and the underpass was built.

The underpass has been a favorite of Shades Cahaba students for a long time. It's 7 ft. tall, 7 ft. wide, and 111 ft. long. There are drainage grates at both ends of the entrance of the tunnel.

I have had a love-hate relationship with the underpass. Most of the time of its existence, it was a dark, smelly place. I would ride my bike through the tunnel and pray I wouldn't run over someone sleeping in there. I have no reason to believe anyone slept in there, but it was kind of creepy. Riding through the dark tunnel on your bicycle at full speed was a right-of-passage for all the boys at Shades Cahaba.

Keeping the tunnel free of trash and graffiti has been an ongoing battle. Lee Seitz, a former student, wrote to me early on with his underpass memories. Back when he was in 3rd grade during the 1979-1980 school year, the art teacher and her classes made the tunnel an art project. They did initial sketches on paper then divided the tunnel walls into sections, and they painted flowers over several class periods. How great must it have been for the kids to see their work every day as they walked to the school.

A mere six years later in 1986, the gangster movie Verne Miller, starring Scott Glenn, shot scenes at the underpass. Unfortunately, they had to paint over all the work to get the shot they needed.

After doing more research on the underpass, it seems the tunnel was painted multiple times. During Principal Sue Grogan's time at Shades Cahaba, they had another art project all because of vandalism. Grogan said, "we were beginning to have problems with graffiti. Of course, that is just a draw for somebody that would like to spray paint something in public because you can do it very secretive at night. One of the jobs that I ask Philip Garner, who was the employee that helped us with the building and as far as maintenance or construction plans and that kind of thing, I always ask him, would you please check the tunnel or underpass every morning before the kids walked to school in case there's something that needs to be covered up? And it was not uncommon."

Grogan spoke with art teacher Mary Jane Coker about turning the tunnel into a project. They brainstormed about what piece of art might discourage the vandals. She said, "Ms. Coker had a group of fourth and fifth graders who did special proj-

The underpass traveling west towards Piggly-Wiggly

ects in the community or at the school. And they did their research on appropriate artwork, large, bold pieces, not intricate, but kind of a folk art look that would be easy to paint on concrete and in a tunnel and bright colors that would discourage folks from harming those walls. I guess it took probably two or three Saturdays for them to go and outline the design that they had planned and then to paint it. It was a real boost, and everybody had it. Even if you didn't walk that way home or if you are a car rider, everybody had a chance to go and take a look."

Today the underpass is probably in the best condition it has ever been in. There are bright lights powered by a solar panel. The walls are painted gray, and yellow safety paint covers the roof, possibly a warning for the tallest walkers. Years ago, someone had the bright idea to pave the walkway. Mercifully the pavement was scraped away, and the smell is gone. There is also talk of the walls getting a new fresh design. This is a good time to visit the underpass.

THE CUBAN MISSILE CRISIS

When I was producing the Shades Cahaba Oral History Project podcast, I asked listeners to send me their stories. Cindy Wise sent me a story to publish about her experience at Shades Cahaba during the Cuban Missile Crisis. This is her story.

In 1962, I was a 3rd grader at Shades Cahaba Elementary School in Homewood, Alabama. The school was directly across from our house on Poinciana Drive. Back in those days, a person, as far as I know, a man only, could open a store charge account at the large downtown Birmingham department stores. As we made selections for purchase, my mother would give the store clerk our name and address, and a bill for the merchandise would be sent to our home later for payment. I can still hear my mother spelling our street name to the clerks in a sing songy voice, P O I N C I A N A.

The school itself was a large building of dark red brick. Inside there were wooden floors. Most of the school's interior walls were painted with that institutional green that we all remember. There was a formal entrance on the front side, and a large ball field in the rear, which is the side our house was on. The building is still used as a public school to this day, and the exterior remains quite similar to the way it looked in the 1960s, though I am sure the interior has had a major renovation.

In third grade, I had my favorite teacher ever, Mrs. Alderson. She was a steady presence with a sweet and caring nature. The class responded to her by behaving and doing our work. I don't remember any discipline problems in Mrs. Alderson's third-grade classroom.

As my third-grade year began, an international crisis broke out, known as the Cuban Missile Crisis. In retaliation for an unsuccessful U.S. led invasion of Cuba in 1961 known as The Bay of Pigs, Cuba's Fidel Castro agreed to allow the Soviet Union to deploy nuclear missiles in Cuba, close to America's southern states. On the Soviet Union's part, this deployment was in response to the U.S.'s deployment of missiles in Turkey and Italy. All of this bluster was a part of the Cold War between the U.S. and the Soviet Union, which began after World War II and ended after the fall of the Berlin Wall in 1989. It's remarkable now to look back at how the Cold War informed our thinking as a nation during my childhood. I guess international terrorism will be the dominant political theme of our current young adults' memories. Of all the international and national current events of my childhood, the Cuban Missile Crisis affected me the most on a personal level.

The first thing that told us that something was amiss was the enactment of bomb drills at school. A specific series of bell rings, different from the bell rings used for a fire drill, indicated it was time to practice for a bomb attack. We would all immediately crouch under our wood and metal desks, whose tops had been scratched up by generations of students before us. And we opened up one of our heavy books and placed it over our heads for additional protection. At the time, I just found this to be interesting and a fun break from school work. I didn't think about how ludicrous this activity was against a nuclear bomb. But we did practice this drill pretty routinely. The correct series of bells would ring, and down to the floor, we would go. Once, the teachers got confused by the bell pattern and filed us out to the field behind the school as we would do for a fire drill. The principal came out excitedly and began to vigorously wave us all back in. We sprinted it-after all, what if this time was the big one?

The next thing that happened was that we were all requested to bring a gallon of water to school in an empty but unrinsed bleach bottle. This was to provide us with sanitary water while we awaited a rescue of some sort after the bomb attack, I assumed. I couldn't remember if bleach bottles made at that time were brown glass or plastic, but a quick google did tell me that bleach came in white plastic bottles by 1962. I do often wonder what happened to all those hundreds of bleach bottles full of water. Are they still stored in a musty basement at the school? Were they removed decades later by people who were clueless as to why they were there? I'll never know.

But the most exciting thing that happened to me during the Cuban Missile Crisis was getting dog tags. The tags were imprinted with our names, our parents' name, our address and date of birth, and an initial indicating our religious affiliation. Mine said P for Protestant. Forms to order dog tags were sent home, and parents had to pay perhaps one or two dollars to have their children tagged in case of a nuclear holocaust. Of course, back then, I never wondered how the silver metal tag with the beaded chain and the barrel clasp would survive the destruction. I just knew that I loved my dog tag. We all painted the embossed lettering with fingernail polish, then, we cleaned up the unembossed portion of the tag with fingernail polish remover, to create the effect of colored lettering. I don't believe then that I understood the purpose of the tags was for the identification of our bodies after a nuclear attack. It all seemed like a lark to me. To a nine year old, those dog tags were a great fashion accessory. They felt like a status symbol. They seemed fancy and special, and I wore them proudly. But how did our parents feel about these events? I can only imagine that these dangerous times caused great anxiety. But my parents never showed any fear or anxiety in front of us kids.

In late October of 1962, the Cuban Missile Crisis ended with the U.S. and the Soviet Union reaching a compromise agreement where both sides agreed to remove their respective missiles, and things calmed down. I believe I still have my dog tag somewhere in my house; I just don't know where. My husband still has his. Before school ended that year, my teacher Mrs. Alderson lost her young adult son to leukemia. I remember being scared that she wouldn't be the same when she returned to school after his death, but she was still the same sweet and caring person, though she was sad and not vivacious. As an adult, I can empathize with how sad and difficult finishing the 1962-63 school year must have been for her. To me, 3rd grade was fun, interesting, memorable, and at times, quite sad.

~ Cindy Reneau Wise

Cindy attended All Saints Episcopal School for kindergarten and first grade. She went to Shades Cahaba from second through sixth grade starting fall of 1961 and finishing sixth grade in spring of 1966. Eight short months after sending me this story, Cindy passed away from cancer on May 28, 2020.

The safety patrol in the 1970s

CHAPTER FOURTEEN

Integration at Shades Cahaba

THE SUPREME COURT RULED in Brown v. Board of Education that segregated schools were unconstitutional in 1954. Thirteen years later, Birmingham area schools were still largely segregated. This letter to parents of students in Jefferson County, dated May 1, 1967, mirrors the exact language of a federal court mandate to eliminate school segregation. Integration would change the face of Shades Cahaba Elementary schools, not to mention schools throughout the county.

Dear Parent:

All grades in our school system will be desegregated next year. Any student who will be entering one of these grades next year may choose to attend any school in our system, regardless of whether that school was formerly all-white or all-negro. It does not matter which school your child is attending this year. You and your child may select any school you wish.

Every student, white and negro, must make a choice of schools. If a child is entering the ninth or higher grade, or if the child is fifteen years old or older, he may make the choice himself. Otherwise, a parent or other adult serving as parent must sign the choice form. A child enrolling in the school system for the first time must make a choice of schools before or at the time of his enrollment.

The form on which the choice should be made is attached to this letter. If should be completed and returned by June 1, 1967. You may mail it, or deliver it by messenger or by hand to any school principal or to the Office of Superintendent at any time between May 1 and June 1. No one may require you to return your choice form before June 1, and no preference is given for returning the choice form early.

No principal, teacher, or other school official is permitted to influence anyone in making a choice or to require early return of the choice form. No one is permitted to favor or penalize any student or other person because of a choice made. A choice once made cannot be changed except for serious hardship.

No child will be denied his choice unless for reasons of overcrowding at the school chosen, in which case children living nearest the school will have preference.

Transportation will be provided, if reasonably possible, no matter what school is chosen. (A child living two miles or more from the nearest school in which his grade is taught, regardless of race, color or national origin, will be eligible for transportation to such school).

Your school board and the school staff will do everything we can to see to it that the rights of all students are protected.

Sincerely yours,

Kermit A. Johnson
Superintendent

HERMAN MAXWELL

When I first started the Shades Cahaba Oral History Project, Herman Maxwell reached out to me with a story he wanted to share. What was his story? "Well, back in the 1967-1968 school year, I was in the fifth grade, and I was one of the first black children to integrate elementary schools in the State of Alabama," Herman told me.

Herman Maxwell grew up in the Rosedale community and had family roots there going back years. "I went to school at Rosedale," he said. "Rosedale was the black school. It was a high school, but it went from the 1st to the 12th grade. My sister attended Rosedale for 11 years, and she was a straight-A student," he said. "She ended up graduating from Shades Valley with honors the year before I went to Shades Cahaba."

School never ended for Herman. "Every year before I would go to the next grade, all summer, I

Herman and a few of his classmates

worked on the subjects that I would be taking the next year. So when I got to that grade, I was ready for what I was getting ready to do." And his family had certain expectations. "My grandmother was an English teacher. My mother was a nurse. My father was a dental hygienist. His twin brother was a chemist. I had several aunties that were educators, and they always told me these words, 'you are a Maxwell, and that means something. We expect more out of you.'"

Moving to Shades Cahaba was not difficult academically for him. "I got a very good education at Rosedale. They taught great fundamentals from the first to the fourth grade. So really, when I got to the fifth grade at Shades Cahaba, I was right in line with everything and lucked out."

"I was a fairly smart kid. It wasn't hard for me to catch on. You know, I was just as smart as anybody in my class." And when Herman looks back and compares the two schools, "At that time, I think the teaching in Rosedale and the teaching at Shades Cahaba were kind of on the same page. Because like I said, I had some great teachers from the first to fourth grades who were dedicated, were educators, and would not take anything but your best."

Herman had a pretty seamless transition from Rosedale to Shades Cahaba, but it was a different story for his sister, who would spend her Senior year at Shades Valley High School. "Well, there was still pushback. My sister caught hell at Shades Valley, and her friends caught hell because nobody wanted them. They put up with a whole lot of stuff that I'd never put up with."

I wondered how she handled it, being only 17 years old. "She just she endured," said Herman." She knew that what she was doing had a purpose and that she was the first. So she had to stand and stay. She was in the band, and at Rosedale, she was in the honor society, and they would not even acknowledge that at Shades Valley."

Did she have any reservations about leaving what she knew to be a good school? Herman said, "It wasn't up to her, it was up to my mother. My mother said, 'we will integrate schools because you have got to get the best education that you possibly can. And in order for you to do that, you must be exposed to other things.' And we knew the disparity between the education that Rosedale versus the education at the white schools."

"The law says separate but equal," said Herman, "and there was no equality whatsoever. I mean, all of the books that they had at Rosedale were secondhand. Five or six years old from the newest version that they had in white schools. But the teachers made do, because, like I said, they were real educators, and they went the extra mile to make sure that they taught the kids what they needed to know."

During the 1960s, Birmingham was ground zero for the civil rights movement. For those who were working for civil rights to those who were trying to keep the status quo. Herman and I talked about the mountain separating the city of Birmingham from Homewood. It almost seemed as if the mountain was a shield, isolating us from the worst of it. Not that things were perfect, just different.

"But the thing of it was, here in Homewood, we didn't have those issues that they had in Birmingham. Well, I mean, yes, there was a certain amount of prejudice that existed. But for the most part, we've always gotten along. I never had a problem coming up in downtown Homewood and stuff like that."

"But I guess, like you said, the mountain might have had a lot to do with it because people on this side of the mountain didn't entertain that foolishness. It was like, you've got white and black. But we are all still just people, it ain't as big a deal, as long as you're trying to do what was right and you're trying to be a good person, then, hey, I'm fine with you. Which was pretty much what transpired, you know what I'm saying?

"I've got friends from the fifth grade that are still my friends today. We were good friends all the way through high school. We keep up with each other. I am a pastor at a church, and I do internet broadcasts. A bunch of my high school friends watch my internet broadcast. And you know, we are still part of each other's lives via social media. And we still get together. I was part of the first Homewood state high school championship football team, and we still get together from time to time."

"Like I said when we met as kids in the fifth grade. We were friends from that day forward, and there was never any of that foolishness between us."

So what did Herman's mother think this whole time? "Well, there were still reservations there. My mom, she was really guarded. But she loosened up as time went on." She sent her children off to pave the way at Shades Valley High School and Shades Cahaba Elementary School, but she was still watching out for them the whole time. "Exactly!" said Herman.

Walking into class on the first day must have felt odd. "It felt just like the first day of fourth grade at Rosedale." Herman said. "Of course, a lot of the kids had never really been around anybody black, in that close proximity. You know, it's not that they hadn't seen black people before, they never had to deal with black people like that before. It wasn't awkward to meet. My teacher was Mrs. Allen, and when I came into the room, she introduced me to everybody. 'This is Herman Maxwell. He's a new student here. We're going to make him feel welcome.'" She said.

Herman wasn't the only black student at Shades Cahaba. "Well, in that particular homeroom, I was. There were several other black students that went there. There were probably ten or twelve kids out of my neighborhood and then maybe 20 or 30 more that got bused in from West Homewood and Mason City that first year."

Then Herman tells me. "I got in one fight that first year, over name-calling." Not everything was perfect for Herman. "I got sent to the principal's office, though, you know, I was always a pretty big kid. I was taller than the principal was, and she was talking about paddling me. And I told her that no ma'am you are not going to paddle me, she said 'I've got to punish you.' I said ma'am, you better call my momma, because if you try to put that paddle on me, you and I are going to be in this office fighting." Herman's mother came to the school and asked what happened. "I said he called me out of my name, and you told me what to do in that circumstance."

"She told the principal 'I'd advise you however you want to do it. Get the teachers to do it. Make your announcement and let them know that if they call him out his name, what the consequences are gonna be. Now, he's not going to just start stuff, but for that, oh, it's gonna be a problem.' And that was the only time I ever had a problem."

Herman felt the academic expectations for the black children were pretty low. "And I blew it out of the water because I was an A student. So after she saw I was just as smart as the white children. Mrs. Allen took a special interest in me, and like I said, she was always from day one, very nice to me, and I've never forgotten that."

Before I spoke to Herman, I had talked with another teacher who was there when the schools were integrated. She also told me how seamless it was and the kids and the parents didn't have a problem. They just got on with business.

Herman feels integration started in Rosedale a few years before he entered Shades Cahaba. "Let's say this was like a process that started a couple of years before my sister went to Shades Valley. With blacks and whites coming together to talk about integration. How is this going to happen and what are we going to do to make sure it goes over as well as it can. It was a concerted effort to make it a smooth transition for us, now in the Birmingham school system, it didn't go quite that smooth. But for us, it was a smooth transition."

Herman summed it up. "And like I said, I got a great education there. I had a smooth transition into integration there. All of us were kids, and we just acted like kids, you ain't going to like everybody. But Shades Cahaba was a launching pad for me educationally, and I'll never forget the start that I got there. I'm proud to say that I came through Shades Cahaba."

MICHAEL GROSS ON INTEGRATION

Herman Maxwell had a great perspective as a student when Homewood integrated. For an administrator's perspective, I spoke with Michael Gross, who was at Homewood Junior High during the school integration. He told me;

"The students at Homewood Junior High and the students at Rosedale, they knew each other. They played park ball together and knew each other in the community. So it wasn't like stranger meeting stranger. We talked to our kids and our parents, no problems. And the Jefferson County School Board let me go over and talk to the Rosedale kids, and we told them what we're going to do. You know, those were back in the days where you had to buy your own books, and it was tough on those kids. And of course, Dr. Foster was really helping at that time. And even after we became a system in 1970, you had to help get them caught up. Not a lot of them. But they had to have books, we had to get books for them. It was very smooth, and they fit right in. And all the athletic teams and the band and the other activities, it just wasn't any real big problems to speak of. You know, you're going to have problems with anything, but there wasn't anything real significant, it went really smooth."

The leadership in Homewood got out in front of any issues which might have come up. Gross said, "When you have Dr. Mamie Foster, and you have a Bob Waldrop as Mayor, and you have other leaders in the council, in the school system, you're not going to have those kinds of problems."

CHAPTER FIFTEEN

Homewood Starts It's Own School System

HOMEWOOD CONTRIBUTED FINANCIALLY to the schools within its city limits while they were part of the Jefferson County School System. Homewood always felt the county underestimated those schools' needs, and they had to step in and make up the difference time and time again.

The City of Homewood had considered having a school system as far back as June 1930. The Mayor and City Attorney consulted with the State Superintendent of Education and the Governor and went so far as to create a school board. The city ultimately decided to stay with the county system later in the year.

In 1944, Homewood sued the Jefferson County Board of Education to recoup money that the city had spent on school improvements during the depression. They won, and Homewood was paid back in installments over the next twenty years with the understanding that if Homewood started an independent system during that time, the debt would be canceled. It wasn't until the late 1960s before Homewood began to look into creating an independent system again. Coincidentally, the debt had been repaid to Homewood.

Michael Gross in the Patriot Lounge

Michael Gross went to work at Homewood Junior High School in 1964, first as a teacher, then assistant principal, and finally principal. When the school system started, he was chosen as the first principal of Homewood High School.

Gross said, "We would not have been a school system if it wasn't for the parents and citizens of the city of Homewood. They wanted something better for their kids. They want their kids to be in an atmosphere where most of them will probably go to college or prepare them for life."

For years there had been issues between Homewood and Jefferson County Schools. Homewood citizens had been paying more in taxes to the county than what they were getting back in services, and there was a sizable student-teacher ratio which parents did not like. Situations kept coming up, and it made people start thinking again about an independent school system in Homewood. "I was an administrator at Homewood Junior High, and a couple of parents came to see me." Gross said. "All the Jefferson County schools had P.T.A., and they went down to the state P.T.A. meeting. The money that the parents were raising wasn't coming back to the schools. They came to see me, went to see the mayor, and went to see the city council. Now, that's just one phase."

The city hired a consultant to see if the citizens would support a millage tax large enough to support the school system. They concluded that Homewood would and could support the tax.

The Homewood City Council established the Homewood Board of Education on December 22, 1969. The board assumed authority on July 1, 1970, with board members Dr. Leslie Wright, Madison W. O'Kelley, Jack R. Gurley, Richard T. Owens, and Mamie Foster. They hired G. Virgil Nunn as the first superintendent, who previously had been superintendent of the Fairfield City Schools.

Homewood officials had offered to purchase Shades Valley High School, but the Jefferson County Board of Education refused to sell. Homewood voters went to the polls on May 25, 1971, to vote on a 5-mill property tax earmarked for construction of a new high school and additional funds to maintain the other schools.

Edgewood Elementary, Hall Kent Elementary, Shades Cahaba Elementary, and Homewood Junior High School would be part of the new school system. Rosedale School, which had closed down a few years before, would stay with the county schools. About 2,500 students transferred to the new school system.

The city had to create a new school system from scratch. Gross said, "There was no school system office. The first office was set up in City Hall, and we had to find out what teachers wanted to stay with Homewood, and who would remain with the county. And that was part of a court order. Teachers had a choice. All the elementary principals at that time went on to stay with the county. I was the principal of the junior high, and I wanted to stay with Homewood." The new superintendent, Virgil Nunn, was very busy. "He had to interview for the elementary principals, he had to work with the city about the finances, and then get the high school built."

The city swapped city-owned land with 15 acres of Samford University land. Homewood then purchased an additional ten acres, all along South Lakeshore Drive. "Of course, that was part of a lakebed, so they had to fill it in. There was also a penalty clause. The contractor had to build the school in a certain time, and

Mr. Nunn, he wasn't going to build a second rate high school. He wanted the best of the best for the kids, and the school system didn't have enough money. Now, it was going to be about a six million dollar building, and that's a lot of money back then. The school system only had about half that amount. The school board and Mr. Nunn went to the city, and the city said we will finance the rest of the money to get the kind of high school you want."

It took a lot of people working together to get the school off the ground. Gross was very complimentary. "We had a great school board and a great council. Everybody was supportive of the school. Everyone was excited."

The court order giving the city permission to start a school system laid out some rules they had to follow. Gross explained. "The court order said we had to pick up a grade each year, so we started with grades K through 9. So instead of the tenth graders going to Shades Valley, we added a grade. Then we added the 11th grade the next year until got to the seniors. We had a junior high building that may have had grades 7 through 9, and then 7 through 10, then 7 through 11. And finally, our seniors were to come back from Shades Valley. "

The first Homewood senior class had been at Shades Valley the entire time. Now they were seniors, and they wouldn't graduate from Shades Valley. Needless to say, they were very upset. Gross did his best to smooth things over for his new seniors.

"Frank Peak was the principal of Shades Valley, and he was very cooperative. He made the kids available and the information I needed about the kids, everything. He cooperated very well." Gross continued. "I had a meeting in the junior high gym for the parents and the kids. The parents weren't upset, but the kids were. We had no colors; we had no mascots; we had no rules and regulations; we had nothing."

Gross leaned on his seniors, and with a lot of guidance, let the high school age students vote on what mascot they wanted and the school colors. Gross said, "almost 90 percent voted Patriots, and the colors, red, white and blue. And we let the kids do that."

That lead to designing the band uniforms and other Patriot items. Next came rules and regulations. One of the first things the seniors wanted was a smoking pit. Jefferson County Schools let students go to a smoking area with parent's permission. The seniors wanted the same privileges at the new school. How did Michael Gross feel about that? "I said, nope, not going to do it." Gross was very health conscientious, and he was not going to let his students smoke.

MAKING ROOM AT THE JUNIOR HIGH

At the start of school in 1972, Homewood still didn't have a completed high school building, and the court order that called for the removal of a grade each year from Shades Valley made the junior high campus more and more crowded. Room needed to be found for three additional grades of students. "The churches were very helpful." Gross said. "At Dawson Memorial Baptist Church, we had the seniors there, and they went back and forth to the junior high building. And the eighth graders were at Trinity United Methodist Church, and they went back and forth. The elementary schools hosted grades K through 7 in the fall. Every school was overcrowded, but it was only supposed to last a semester until the high school was ready to open up."

Before the new school opened for students, the school Christmas program was held in the new high school auditorium. Equipment and desks would be moved in over the holidays so the seniors could finish out the last half of their year at the new high school. One problem, Gross needed help. "In December, when the school was turned over to us, they were dropping off all the desks and equipment for the school, and I had no way to move it in. The seniors were about to go to exams, and I gave them a choice. Do you want to help me move the furniture in and you won't take your final exams? And it was 100 percent of them. Not only that, but they also helped me during the holidays to move it in."

This move was felt at Shades Cahaba and all the schools in the Homewood system. Grades 1-7 were at the elementary schools during the fall. When Home-wood High School opened its doors to grades 9-12 in January 1973, grades 6-7 would leave the elementary schools soon after. The Junior High School would house grades 6-8 and eventually change its name to Homewood Middle School to reflect the grade change. The elementary schools would become grades 1-5, and for the first time, Shades Cahaba would truly become an elementary school five decades after it first opened its doors.

CHAPTER SIXTEEN

Shades Cahaba in the 21st Century

THE FIRST EPISODE OF THE PODCAST, The Shades Cahaba Oral History Project, was a conversation with current Shades Cahaba Principal John Lowry. We talked about the beginnings of Shades Cahaba, and I asked him to tell me what Shades Cahaba looks like today, as it is starting its second century as a school.

When we spoke in the fall of 2019, Lowry told me, "Right now, we have 506 students. That is small for us. We have gone down in size the past three years roughly." He said, "We peaked about the 2015-16 school year when we had close to 560 kids. There was a time before I got here where we bumped up against 600 for a couple of years. We've had a bubble of kids come through and, we've dropped back down to what this building was intended to house."

Since the days the doors opened at Shades Cahaba, the parents have been a vital part of the growth of the school. It started with the School Improvement Association, which became the Parent Teacher Association (P.T.A.). It is now known as the Parent Teacher Organization (P.T.O.). I spoke with the 2019-2020

P.T.O. President Alexa McElroy about how they continue to support the school.

"Yes, the spirit lives on. In fact, we just provided all of the new furniture for our renovated library," said Alexa. Projects change due to the school's needs, and she told me about what they were working on that year.

"We have one fundraiser each year, and that is our winter festival held in February of each year." She said, "Through our corporate sponsorships for this event, our silent auction ticket sales and our Owl-mazing Race, with that money, we can do things like provide classroom assistance, which we give the school over the summer. The money is distributed to the teachers to use as they wish in their classrooms. And we have room in our budget each year for additional teacher grants. Teachers can submit applications to the P.T.O. for anything that they might additionally need for their classrooms, be it any resource, flexible seating; we see a little bit of everything. And we provide that support for our teachers."

A SCHOOL OF CHARACTER

Sue Grogan came to Shades Cahaba in 1988 and became the principal in 2000. She saw an opportunity to help guide the staff and students

"I was fortunate to be able to work with wonderful, wonderful teachers and parents who sent their children through the doors of Shades Cahaba every day with the wish that not only would they be educated academically, but they would be taught right living." Sue said, "I had a group of young teachers that after they got their feet wet in the classroom and had a good rhythm with their instruction, they began to talk about what they were seeing with the children of the time."

"Those children that were making good choices and those children that from time to time, as all children do, make a choice that would serve them better if they had chosen something else." The teachers came to Sue and said that they would like to start a character education program, an intentional one.

"Now, all good schools have rules and expectations and an interest to raise children that make good choices, have strong characters, and are respectful, responsible children. But I really appreciated these young teachers coming and saying; I think there are some things that we can be intentional about. And that's how it started from the grassroots."

"When things are very effective in the life of a school, is when it's not top-down. When it comes from the folks that are working with those children eight hours a day in a classroom. At about the same time, Melinda Hollingsworth, who was the extended day director, came to me and was interested in helping children make good choices after school. She had them from 3 pm until 6 pm in our extended day program. She brought a list of, not rules, but expectations. They were the cornerstones from a previous experience that she had working with children. We took a look at them, tweaked them a little bit, and they became our Shades Cahaba Way. Six expectations.

"The thing that is different about them is that they are very positive. Things like take charge of yourself. You're responsible for you. Avoid put-downs. Who needs them? The last one is Have fun, life is a gift, and that is not usually a school rule. And I think when we started having that common language, the children grasped it; they embraced it."

"The faculty and staff embraced it. The parents embraced it. And then it started going out into the community. That's the first place that we started with our intentional common language, through the Shades Cahaba Way. And then it just took off from there. There are so many examples of how the character education program flourished at Shades Cahaba."

"One example is the way our custodial staff embraced the Shades Cahaba Way. Rather than calling them the custodial staff, we called them the caretakers, which is a nice welcoming title for them because they certainly took care of not only the building but all of us."

"We then gave them the responsibility of naming a best nest classroom once a week. That classroom that intentionally took care of their room, they'd pick up trash. They would keep their desk in order, put their chairs up so that the caretaker could come in and clean the floors easily. And then they had a banner that they could hang outside their door as the 'best nest.' So everybody embraced it in their own way. And it became systemic and culture changing for us.

Sue had been in the building for 13 years and had never had a leadership role before she was appointed principal. She decided to lean on the experience in the staff around her.

"I wanted to make sure that I was intentional with the choices that I made, while I was expecting everyone else to be intentional with their choices. I decided that I needed, not a management team, which is very common in school associations and in school buildings. But I needed a leadership team."

"I told my faculty and staff that I was happy to do the management part of the job. But because it was not just my school, it was our school that I needed people with a vision of where they wanted this place to go for children. And so at the end of my first year at our faculty meeting, as we were wrapping up the year, I asked them to vote for six teacher leaders, teachers that they felt would lead our school in a positive place. Organizations don't just stay the same. They either decline, or they improve. And I wanted our story to be that of improvement. So they elected six teachers, and we added a staff member, a support staff member, and we added a parent on that visionary team. Instead of leadership team, we named it visionary, and we had our own mission statement. I made sure that everyone realized that if there was a problem with the ice cream box in the lunchroom line or the gym floor, they needed to come to me and not bother the teacher leaders about that. But if they had an idea of how to make instruction better or the culture of the school better, that's who they needed to approach. One of us on the visionary team."

The Visionary team started making yearly goals that the teachers would work toward. Sue said, "it might be math, it might be science, it might be language arts, but we also had a goal that was something about our culture."

"And then we put a little bit of money behind that so that we could support it financially and we'd have some resources that we could use or some professional development that we could use. So when you start putting all those components together, where you've got the voice of faculty and staff and parents and children, and you have goals that you write, and then you put some money behind it and some effort behind it, wonderful things happen."

Current Principal John Lowry has continued to promote the Shades Cahaba Way. "Everybody that has been in this building in the past 18 years knows what the Shades Cahaba Way is. It's a group of six statements that define what we expect for everybody. An organization called Character.org recognizes schools around the nation for their character practices and character programs, and our Shades Cahaba Way earned what was called a promising practice. In 2004, we applied for a National School of Character through character.org, and in 2006, Shades Cahaba was recognized as a National School of Character. I think there were thirty-eight other schools in the country that were recognized. The designation is good for about five years, so in 2011, we reapplied and were designated a 2012 National School of Character. In 2017 we applied again for the third time and were recognized again."

"We've learned that the application process that we go through gives us a lot of information about how we're doing. And that's the benefit of doing it. And it's nice that they recognize that we've got some good things happening in the building. But the good part of it is the process of investigating what you're doing, getting feedback about that, and then trying to improve. So we've had it go pretty well for us."

The National School of Character is not the only recognition Shades Cahaba has received. Lowry said, "In 2015, for the second time, Shades Cahaba was recognized as a Blue Ribbon School of Excellence. We were one of five schools in Alabama that year. That's not an application thing. We just got a nice email saying, hey, you're going to be one of them for this year. So we were pleased about that."

As a new parent at Shades Cahaba, you are exposed to the Shades Cahaba Way early on, and you often hear about it. As your kids make their way through school, you can see the benefits of learning and living the Shades Cahaba Way through their actions. I feel it pays off when the kids get to middle school because it can be a tough place for some kids. They have been taught you do things a certain way, treat people a certain way, and see the impact it has on them.

Lowry explained. "Yeah, there's definitely some truth in the repetition that comes along with that. The kindergartners hear it, and I talk about it every day on the announcements. By the time they leave here in six years, if they don't know it, it's because they weren't listening because we sure talk about it a good bit. But I do think that repetition does pay off down the road because the kids remember it, and we've had lots of kids come back to visit, and they remember the Shades Cahaba Way."

A THANKSGIVING STORY

This book is full of stories about how the community has supported the school. To finish the book, I wanted to share one more story Sue Grogan shared with me during her time at Shades Cahaba.

"One of my favorite times of the year, personally, is Thanksgiving. That's just my favorite holiday, and I love the whole feeling of being grateful for blessings. Dr. Cleveland came up with a wonderful idea for the Homewood schools to honor our community helpers during that season of Thanksgiving. He asked Shades Cahaba to be the first school to do this. So on the week before the Thanksgiving holidays, we set out invitations to everyone who worked in the community helping us, such as the first responders, fire department and the police department, our city council, government, street and sanitation workers, anybody that helped us. We asked them to come and join us for our Thanksgiving meal. We did ask for reservations so that we'd kind of have an idea of how many would come. I asked our children to help host and hostess our visitors. So I had a whole group of kids from kindergarten through fifth grade that would be in the lobby waiting for the guests to come through. A school lunch line can be a little confusing, but even if you have a five-year-old with you, they can show you how to go through it."

"And then we also set up an area, a luncheon area in our media center. I also had the children who met them to go ahead and get their lunch so that they could sit and eat with our guests. One of my favorite stories from the first time that we did that was, I had a kindergartner come and ask me 'Can I take my guests back to my room? I want to introduce them to my friends.' And I said 'If he has time and if he would like to, of course, you may.' He was one of our street and sanitation workers, and of course, none of them went home and got dressed for this. They came in their work clothes. And I believe he had even brought the truck because he didn't have a long period of time for lunch, so the truck was sitting out in the driveway. He goes back to the kindergarten class and talks about his job, and the kids are fascinated. They've never spoken to someone who helps us with our trash control, and he described the truck. I believe they even went out and took a look at it and, you know, and he made it work for them. Well, out of that came a wonderful friendship of this little boy and the gentleman who happened to have the route where the little boy lived. And there were stories throughout the years of how, especially in the summer, the boy would sit on his front steps and wait for him to come by, and they would speak and say hello."

"Is that a meal from the lunchroom? Yes, but oh my goodness, so much richer than just the food on the plate. It was the time of enjoying that meal with a new friend."

I was happy to see that this past Thanksgiving, the school was still sharing a meal with our community helpers.

The back of the school.

CHAPTER SEVENTEEN

The Second 100 Years

YOU MIGHT THINK THIS BOOK is about a building, a building which has stood for 100 years. You would be right, but not completely. This book is about the students and teachers who have spent time in its hallowed walls. It's about the parents who have given of themselves and the people in the community, who may have never set foot inside the building, but who have fought tirelessly for the school to exist and thrive.

As I read and listened to the school's stories during its first one hundred years, the same things kept coming up repeatedly. This community had always valued education for their children, even before we labeled this community Homewood. It didn't matter if the school was held in a log cabin, someone's home, or a consolidated school building. When the school needed help to overcome an obstacle or simply become a better school, the community rallied around it again and again.

The Zelosophian Academy was a good school, but alumni Will Franke and William Acton knew a better school was needed. They led a successful campaign to start a new school to consolidate all the other schools in Shades Valley. Voters approved a special tax to construct Shades Cahaba, and citizens continue to support Shades Cahaba and all the schools in our system to this day.

As soon as Shades Cahaba opened, a new group was formed by parents, the School Improvement Association. These parents supported the school in ways the school budget could not. Just one example was they stocked the library with books to gain the accreditation of the Southern Association of Colleges and Secondary Institutions. Today, this group is called the P.T.O. and continues to back the school, it's teachers, and they continue to stock the library with books and equipment.

During the depression, schools around the state went to either a 6-month calendar or completely shut down to save money. The city of Homewood and it's citizens rallied around the schools and found the funds to keep Shades Cahaba open for the entire school year.

Improvements were made in the 1940s, and when it became apparent a new, larger and more modern high school was needed, area communities, including Homewood, voted for a tax to help construct what became known as Shades Valley High School.

Approximately 20 years later, the citizens of Homewood were asked to support the start of their own school system, which they heartily accepted. The citizen support of this new school system and the individual schools continue to this day, 50 years after it was created.

I am excited for the second century of Shades Cahaba, and hopefully, this time, the owl is there for good.

I'll let Homewood School Superintendent Bill Cleveland have the last word:

"Like I said, this didn't just happen, we're standing on the shoulders of giants here in this community. And the local involvement, whether it's through giving of time or giving financial resources or other types of resources, continues today. And that example, that was said a long time ago, has served us well."

CHAPTER SEVENTEEN

Appendices

SHADES CAHABA WAS DEDICATED on Labor Day, Monday, September 6, 1920. That afternoon, after the formal addresses and a picnic dinner on the grounds, Mrs. Floribel Brown Ohme, unveiled the "bronze tablets to the soldier boys of Shades-Cahaba." These are two large bronze plaques, mounted on both sides of the auditorium doors, visible as soon as you walked into the new high school.

Both plaques say, "In honor of the boys and girls of this school district who served in the army or navy of the United States of America in the World War 1917-1919."

At the bottom of the plaques, it says, "This tablet is dedicated by the residents of Shades Cahaba High School District 1-A 1919."

The following pages are the names of the individuals split between the two plaques in the school, and I have combined them into one list here. Those who lost their lives have an asterisk after their names.

Arthur Acton

Bernie Acton

Lieutenant Fred Acton

Robert Acton

John Sidney Aldridge

Newton M. Aldridge

O'Neil Alred

Dan Armstrong

John Bailey

Roland Bailey

George Baker

William Baker

Joe Bast

Foy Batson

Alfred Bearden

Curtis Bearden

Fred Bearden

John Bearden*

Robert Bearden

Walter Bearden*

Newton Bohannon

Fritz Bolle

Arthur Brashier

Floyd Brashier

Capt. Francis Brown

Billy Browning

Sam B. Browning

Emmitt Byers

Lummie Caldwell

Captain J. T. Callaway

Joseph Campbell

Jack Carter

Woodson Cates

Willis Clark

Ben Cooper

Robert Cooper

Arthur E. Curl

Walter Curl

Lieut. M. G. Dabney

Andy Dardy

Willie Dawson*

David Denton

Peyton Deshazo

George Despison

Will Dison

David Donahoo

Arthur Duke

Lieut. Edwin Duke

J. Parks Ellenburg

W. H. Ellenberg

Ross W. Ellenberg

James M. Elliott

Clarence Erickson

Lieut. Horvin H. Eubank

Barney Evans

George Evans

Walter Everett

Ernest Fleming

Percy Gambrell

Clarence Good

Paul Goode

Clark R. Goodwin

James Goodwin

John Goodwin

Frank Graham

John Graham

Leonard or a sing

Charlie Griffin

Leslie Griffin

Tom Griffin*

Lonnie Grissom

L. E. Gulledge

Lieut. Allie Hale

Evan Hale

Jack Hanks

Jessie Wisen Harper

John Harper

G. Wyant Hayes

Willie Helm

Lieut. Charles Hewitt

Robert Hewitt

Roy Higgis

Ollie Hitt

Arthur Hodges

Joseph Hodges

Will Hodges

Miss Marion E. Houlihan

Miss Virginia Houlihan

W. Newton Hubbard Jr.

Will Hullette

Emmitt Hunnicutt

Ralph Hunnicutt

Byron Jackson

Lieut. Carl Jackson

Guy Jackson

Coze Jones

Frank Jones

George Jones

Sam Oscar Jones

Hanson Keller

Wesley Kent

Lieut. H. Cecil Kilpatrick

J. Bunion Kilpatrick

J. Devotie Kilpatrick

Paul M. Kilpatrick

Norman Kleindienst

Lieut. Hugh Lester

Frank Limbaugh

Oscar Limbaugh

Grady Lodge

Lester Loggins

Coleman Maske

James Ernest Massey

Jay Melton

Capt. Arthur Merkel

"Pat" Floyd E. McBride

Neil McCloud

Pete McCloud

Manon McSweeney

Henry R Millar

Will T. Millar

James R. Milstead

Barney Moran

Edwin Morris

Otis Murphree

Austin O'Barr

Fred O'Barr

Luther Pardue

Jim Parrish

Tom Partain

Dumas F. Philips

Eldridge Plowman

Will Rasco

Charles Reed

"Dick" Stanton Reese

Hugh M. Reese

George Reynolds

Joe Rigney

Robert Riley

James Pugh Rittenberry

E.J. Salter

George Schmidt

Peter Scott

Raymond Scott

Will Scott

Will Sellers

Pete Shumacher

Howard Simms

H. Conville Sizemore

Anthony Smith

Benjamin Smith

Edgar Smith

J.W. Edward Smith

Lee Smith

Wescott Smith

Burt Tilerson

James Tollett

Harry Tritt

Will Tritt

Cecil Tyler

Clifford Tyler

Hugh Tyler

Luther H. Tyler

Ernest Walker

Walter Walker

Glenn Washington

Nat Washington

Arthur A. Watkins

Tom Watson

Thurber West

J. B. Whaley *

Leon white

Emmitt Wilder

David Williams*

Fred Williams

Truman Williams

Henry Wise

"Jack" D.P. Wilson

Basil Wood

Lieut. Leighton Wood

Capt. Sterling A. Wood, Jr.

G. Thomas Wooten*

James E. Wright

Grady Wyatt

AFTER WORLD WAR II, another plaque was dedicated on Homecoming Day, October 24th, to the boys who lost their lives in World War II. The ceremony included a gun salute, a prayer by an army chaplain and the presentation of the plaque. Those who gave their lives are:

J. C. Bailey

Raymond Earl Bolle

Grover C. Bryant Jr.

Luther Clay

Arthur Cundy

Willy Gautney

Ralph Goodwin

James Graham

Thomas Hope

Jo Earl Hurtt

William Moore McCrary

John McCullough

Robert L. McNutt

Huey McSweeney

R. P. Morris

W. Clem Mulkey

Emory Poe

James Sexton

Clayton Taylor

Harold E. Wehby

George Williams

Menta Edward Witten

Ralph Wyatt

Shades Cahaba High School Football Scores 1921-1949

1921	*Opponent*	*Score*	*Final*	*Game Location*
Fri., Oct. 7	Bessemer	0-56	L	
Sat., Oct. 15	Inter-Church	7-6	W	
Fri., Oct. 21	Jones Valley	35-0	W	
Fri., Nov. 4	Simpson	0-41	L	
Thu., Nov. 10	Woodlawn	14-12	W	
Fri., Nov. 18	Jefferson County	0-39	L	

1922				
Mon., Oct. 9	Bessemer	0-26	L	
Sat., Oct. 14	Walker	0-48	L	
Fri., Nov. 3	Jones Valley	0-0	T	
	Hueytown	0-6	L	
Fri., Nov. 17	Simpson	0-26	L	

1923				
Fri., Sep. 28	Mortimer Jordan	12-0	W	
Fri., Oct. 5	Bessemer	0-13	L	
Fri., Oct. 12	Oak Grove	56-0	W	
	Alliance	21-7	W	
	Five Points	23-0	W	
Sat., Oct. 30	Minor	44-0	W	
Fri., Oct. 26	Simpson	0-7	L	
Fri., Nov. 9	Five Points	0-0	T	
Wed., Nov. 28	Jones Valley	7-6	W	

1924

Fri., Sep. 26	Mortimer Jordan	8-0	W
Fri., Oct. 10	McAdory	26-6	W
Fri., Oct. 17	Bessemer	0-12	L
Thu., Oct. 23	Anniston	0-13	L
Fri., Nov. 7	Simpson	0-18	L
Thu., Nov. 13	University	0-7	L
Fri., Nov. 21	Shelby County	0-32	L
Wed., Nov. 26	Jones Valley	6-31	L

1925

Fri., Oct. 9	Alliance	26-0	W
Sat., Oct. 24	Bibb County	14-0	W
Fri., Oct. 30	Simpson	7-7	T
Sat., Nov. 7	@ Minor	7-2	W
Fri., Nov. 20	University	0-6	L
Wed., Nov. 25	Jones Valley	3-0	W

1926

Fri., Oct. 15	Sylacauga	6-6	T
Fri., Oct. 22	Simpson	0-0	T
Thu., Oct. 28	Bibb County	0-0	T
Fri., Nov. 5	Leeds	27-7	W
Fri., Nov. 12	Dora	6-0	W
Fri., Nov. 19	Chilton County	7-6	W
Wed., Nov. 24	Jones Valley	0-0	T

1927

Fri., Sep. 30	Walker	0-37	L

Sat., Oct. 8	Ensley	0-59	L	
Fri., Oct. 14	Simpson	0-71	L	
Fri., Oct. 21	Greenville	0-12	L	
Fri., Oct. 28	Leeds			
Fri., Nov. 4	Hueytown	0-33	L	
Fri., Nov. 11	Minor	45-7	W	
Fri., Nov. 18	St. Bernard	0-87	L	
Wed., Nov. 23	Jones Valley	12-44	L	

1928

Fri., Sep. 28	Hewitt	12-13	L	
Fri., Oct. 5	Warrior	0-0	T	
Fri., Oct. 12	Simpson	0-53	L	
Fri., Oct. 19	Mortimer Jordan	0-33	L	
Thu., Oct. 25	Paul Hayne	6-7	L	
Fri., Nov. 9	Hueytown	0-32	L	
	Minor	0-6	L	
Fri., Nov. 16	Dora	12-25	L	
Wed., Nov. 28	Jones Valley	6-18	L	

1929

Sat., Sep. 21	Mortimer Jordan	13-0	W	
	@ Hewitt	0-0	T	
Fri., Oct. 11	@ Simpson	6-13	L	Munger Bowl
Fri., Oct. 18	Warrior	28-6	W	
Fri., Oct. 25	Minor	26-0	W	
Sat., Nov. 2	@ Hueytown	13-20	L	
Fri., Nov. 8	@ Woodlawn	6-43	L	Legion Field
Wed., Nov. 27	Jones Valley	0-3	L	

1930

	Hewitt	0-0	T	
Fri., Oct. 10	Simpson	6-13	L	
Fri., Oct. 17	@ Bibb County	6-19	L	
	Minor	20-6	W	
Fri., Oct. 31	Hueytown	6-6	T	
Thu., Nov. 6	Woodlawn	12-0	L	
Fri., Nov. 14	Mortimer Jordan	6-6	T	
Wed., Nov. 26	Jones Valley	7-6	W	

1931

Fri., Sep. 25	@ Jones Valley	12-7	W	Legion Field
Fri., Oct. 2	McAdory	26-0	W	
Thu., Oct. 8	@ Ensley	0-7	L	Legion Field
Fri., Oct. 16	Mortimer Jordan	32-6	W	
Fri., Oct. 23	Bibb County	18-6	W	
Fri., Oct. 30	Hueytown	34-7	W	
Fri., Nov. 6	Hewitt	37-7	W	
Wed., Nov. 11	@ Simpson	38-6	W	Munger Bowl
Fri., Nov. 20	Minor	21-0	W	
Fri., Nov. 26	Pell City	38-6	W	

1932

Fri., Sep. 23	Jones Valley	12-7	W
Fri., Sep. 30	Oak Grove	25-13	W
Fri., Oct. 7	Oxford	7-25	L
Fri., Oct. 14	Leeds	20-0	W
Fri., Oct. 28	Hueytown	0-14	L
Fri., Nov. 4	Mortimer Jordan	6-6	T

Fri., Nov. 11	Minor	13-27	L
Mon., Nov. 21	B.B. Comer	13-27	L

1933

Fri., Sep. 29	Etowah	0-45	L
Fri., Oct. 6	Bibb County	6-0	W
Fri., Oct. 13	Jones Valley	0-13	L
Fri., Oct. 20	Leeds	24-12	W
Fri., Oct. 27	Hueytown	0-12	L
Fri., Nov. 3	Mortimer Jordan	19-6	W
Fri., Nov. 10	Hewitt-Trussville	7-13	L
Fri., Nov. 17	Minor	43-0	W
Fri., Nov. 24	McAdory	6-6	T

1934

Fri., Sep. 28	Bibb County	6-27	L
Fri., Oct. 5	Jones Valley	0-19	L
Fri., Oct. 12	Leeds	18-0	W
Fri., Oct. 19	West Jefferson	12-19	L
Fri., Oct. 26	Hueytown	0-27	L
Fri., Nov. 2	Mortimer Jordan	18-14	W
Fri., Nov. 16	Minor	19-7	W

1935

Fri., Sep. 27	Woodlawn	0-8	L
Thu., Oct. 3	Jones Valley	0-6	L
Fri., Oct. 11	Bibb County	0-7	L
Fri., Oct. 18	West Jefferson	19-6	W
Fri., Oct. 25	Leeds	19-0	W
Fri., Nov. 1	Mortimer Jordan	26-7	W

| Fri., Nov. 8 | Hueytown | 0-7 | L |
| Fri., Nov. 15 | Minor | 6-0 | W |

1936

Fri., Sep. 25	Bibb County	6-0	W
Fri., Oct. 2	Jones Valley	0-18	L
Fri., Oct. 9	Jefferson County	9-12	L
Fri., Oct. 16	West Jefferson	13-0	W
Fri., Oct. 23	Leeds	26-6	W
Fri., Oct. 30	Mortimer Jordan	12-0	W
Fri., Nov. 6	Hueytown	0-6	L
Fri., Nov. 13	Minor	0-7	L
Fri., Nov. 20	Dora	13-19	L

1937

Thu., Sep. 23	Tuscaloosa County	0-32	L
Thu., Sep. 30	Jones Valley	13-0	W
Fri., Oct. 8	Jefferson County	7-19	L
Fri., Oct. 15	West Jefferson	24-6	W
Fri., Oct. 22	Leeds	27-0	W
Fri., Oct. 29	Mortimer Jordan	26-7	W
Fri., Nov. 5	Hueytown	13-21	L
Tue., Nov. 16	Minor	12-0	W
Fri., Nov. 26	West Blocton	6-13	L

1938

Fri., Sep. 23	Tuscaloosa County	12-13	L
Thu., Sep. 29	Jones Valley	22-0	W
Thu., Oct. 6	McAdory	32-6	W

Fri., Oct. 14	West Jefferson	43-0	W
Fri., Oct. 21	Leeds	47-0	W
Fri., Oct. 28	Mortimer Jordan	40-7	W
Mon., Nov. 7	Hueytown	0-14	L
Mon., Nov. 14	Minor	27-0	W
Mon., Nov. 21	Oak Grove	32-0	W

1939

Thu., Sep. 21	West End	7-18	L
Fri., Sep. 29	McAdory	32-0	W
Fri., Oct. 13	Tuscaloosa County	14-6	W
Thu., Oct. 19	Leeds	20-0	W
Fri., Oct. 27	Jones Valley	33-6	W
Thu., Nov. 2	Hueytown	19-0	W
Fri., Nov. 10	Mortimer Jordan	30-6	W
Thu., Nov. 16	Oak Grove	26-8	W
Fri., Nov. 24	Minor	39-0	W

1940

Fri., Sep. 20	West End	13-21	L
Fri., Sep. 27	Oneonta	0-13	L
Fri., Oct. 4	Oak Grove	33-7	W
Fri., Oct. 11	Tuscaloosa County	0-6	L
Fri., Oct. 18	Leeds	12-6	W
Fri., Oct. 25	Jones Valley	13-7	W
Sat., Nov. 2	Hueytown	13-12	W
Fri., Nov. 8	Mortimer Jordan	6-0	W
Thu., Nov. 21	Minor	6-6	T

1941

Sat., Sep. 20	West End	0-28	L	
Fri., Sep. 26	Oneonta	0-13	L	
Fri., Oct. 3	Oak Grove	7-0	W	
Fri., Oct. 10	Tuscaloosa County	0-18	L	
Fri., Oct. 17	Leeds	19-0	W	
Mon., Nov. 3	Hueytown	0-33	L	
Fri., Nov. 7	Mortimer Jordan	26-0	W	
Wed., Nov. 19	Minor	12-0	W	

1942

Fri., Sep. 18	@ West End	0-12	L	Legion Field
Fri., Sep. 25	Oneonta	19-7	W	Ellenburg Field
Fri., Oct. 2	Minor	19-12	W	Ellenburg Field
Fri., Oct. 9	@ Tuscaloosa County	14-13	W	
Fri., Oct. 16	Leeds	45-13	W	Ellenburg Field
Fri., Oct. 23	Jones Valley	12-0	W	Ellenburg Field
Fri., Oct. 30	Hueytown	7-26	L	Ellenburg Field
Fri., Nov. 6	Mortimer Jordan	33-6	W	Ellenburg Field
Thu., Nov. 19	@ Ramsay	7-7	T	Legion Field

1943

Wed., Sep. 22	@ Ramsay	7-6	W	Legion Field
Thu., Sep. 30	Minor	20-0	W	Ellenburg Field
Fri., Oct. 8	Glencoe	19-6	W	Ellenburg Field
Fri., Oct. 15	Leeds	33-7	W	Ellenburg Field
Fri., Oct. 22	Jones Valley	40-0	W	Ellenburg Field
Fri., Oct. 29	@ Hueytown	0-13	L	Hueytown
Fri., Nov. 5	Mortimer Jordan	26-26	T	Ellenburg Field

Fri., Nov. 12	Jefferson County	25-0	W	Ellenburg Field
Fri., Nov. 19	Tuscaloosa County	14-13	W	Ellenburg Field

1944

Wed., Sep. 20	Ramsay	0-33	L
Fri., Sep. 29	Minor	39-6	W
Fri., Oct. 13	Leeds	19-13	W
Fri., Oct. 20	Jones Valley	32-6	W
Fri., Oct. 27	Phillips Birmingham	20-6	W
Thu., Nov. 2	Tuscaloosa County	14-7	W
Fri., Nov. 10	Jefferson County	21-0	W
Fri., Nov. 17	Mortimer Jordan	51-6	W
Thu., Nov. 23	St. Bernard	33-6	W

1945

Thu., Sep. 20	Leeds	33-12	W
Fri., Sep. 28	Minor	38-0	W
Wed., Oct. 3	Woodlawn	12-0	W
Fri., Oct. 12	Hueytown	0-13	L
Fri., Oct. 19	Jones Valley	39-0	W
Fri., Oct. 26	Phillips Birmingham	21-7	W
Fri., Nov. 2	Tuscaloosa County	33-14	W
Fri., Nov. 16	Mortimer Jordan	60-8	W
Thu., Nov. 22	St. Bernard	19-0	W

1946

Fri., Sep. 20	Jones Valley	20-0	W
Fri., Sep. 27	Minor	27-0	W
Thu., Oct. 3	Woodlawn	0-46	W

Fri., Oct. 11	Hueytown	0-6	L
Fri., Oct. 18	Leeds	7-0	W
Fri., Oct. 25	Tuscaloosa County	0-22	L
Fri., Nov. 1	Fairfield	6-12	L
Fri., Nov. 15	Mortimer Jordan	32-12	W
Thu., Nov. 21	St. Bernard	38-12	W

1947

Thu., Sep. 18	Jones Valley	21-6	W
Fri., Sep. 26	Minor	34-6	W
Fri., Oct. 3	Montevallo	38-7	W
Fri., Oct. 10	Hueytown	26-0	W
Fri., Oct. 17	@ Leeds	14-13	W
Fri., Oct. 24	Tuscaloosa County	14-7	W
Sat., Nov. 1	@ Fairfield	20-0	W
Tue., Nov. 11	@ Aliceville	6-18	L
Fri., Nov. 14	Mortimer Jordan	7-0	W
Thu., Nov. 20	St. Bernard	40-13	W

1948

Thu., Sep. 16	Jones Valley	12-19	L
Thu., Sep. 23	Minor	26-14	W
Fri., Oct. 1	John Carroll	13-6	W
Fri., Oct. 8	Hueytown	13-6	W
Fri., Oct. 15	Leeds	31-2	W
Thu., Oct. 21	Tuscaloosa County	6-0	W
Fri., Oct. 29	Fairfield	12-20	L
Thu., Nov. 4	Mortimer Jordan	23-12	W
Thu., Nov. 18	McAdory	0-0	T

Alma Mater

THE OWL YEARBOOK had posted the words to the Shades Cahaba High School Alma Mater, but I had no idea what the tune was. During my interview with Herb Griffin, he was able to sing part of it, and the tune was familiar, very familiar. I had heard it in a movie before. It was the Kellerman's theme sung as a parting song at the end of Dirty Dancing. A little more research and I found out the tune is "Annie Lisle," a song written about a girl who dies of consumption. The song may have faded into oblivion if not for the fact the tune was also adopted by countless colleges, universities, and high schools for their alma mater, including the University of Alabama. As an Auburn University graduate, it slipped right by me. Here are the lyrics.

Hail to thee, our Alma Mater,
    Shades Cahaba High,
From thy sons and from they daughters,
    Hear our battle cry.

From they mountain sides and valleys,
    From the fertile plains,
From our homes and distant places,
    Here we come to train.

May the foes before thee tremble,
    At the Red and Black,
May thy heroes in the struggle,
    Never courage lack.

We will keep thy name in honor,
    Safe from every blight,
In our loss or in our victory,
    Striving for the right.

Chorus —
Faith, loyal, true to thee,
    As the year goes by;
We will ever sing thy praises,
    Shades Cahaba High.

— *H.S. Keller*

Yearbook Locations

ARE YOU LOOKING for a Shades Cahaba High School yearbook? We have found them in these locations.

Year	Physical Location	Online
1921	*We don't believe they produced one for the first year.*	
1922	Linn Henley	
1923	Linn Henley	
1924	Linn Henley	
1925	Missing*	
1926	Linn Henley	
1927	Linn Henley	
1928	Linn Henley	Ancestry.com
1929	Linn Henley	Ancestry.com
1930	Linn Henley	Ancestry.com
1931	Shades Cahaba	Ancestry.com
1932	Shades Cahaba	Ancestry.com
1933	Shades Cahaba	Ancestry.com
1934	Shades Cahaba	Ancestry.com
1935	Shades Cahaba	
1936	Linn Henley	
1937	Linn Henley	
1938	Linn Henley	
1939	—	Ancestry.com
1940	Linn Henley	Ancestry.com
1941	Shades Cahaba	Ancestry.com
1942	Shades Cahaba	Ancestry.com
1943	Linn Henley	Ancestry.com

1944	Shades Cahaba	Ancestry.com
1945	Linn Henley	Ancestry.com
1946	Linn Henley	Ancestry.com
1947	Shades Cahaba	Ancestry.com
1948	Linn Henley	Ancestry.com
1949	Linn Henley	Ancestry.com
1950**	Shades Cahaba	
1951**	Shades Cahaba	

- Linn Henley Research Library is located in the original Birmingham Public Library on the corner of Linn Park.
- If you have an Ancestry.com account, you can access yearbooks by searching U.S., School Yearbooks, 1900-1999.
- Shades Cahaba yearbooks are in possession of the school principal.
- Shades Valley High School has a copy of the 1929 and 1930 yearbooks.
* If you happen to have a copy of the 1925 Shades Cahaba Owl Yearbook, consider donating it to the Linn Henley Research Library to be kept with the others. The same goes for years 1931, 1932, 1933, 1934, 1935, 1939, 1941, 1942, 1944, 1947.
** The 1950 and 1951 yearbooks were produced for the Junior High Students still located at Shades Cahaba.

The Shades Cahaba Way

THE SHADES CAHABA STUDENT POPULATION is a diverse one, adding a uniqueness to the school community. The school has a high academic standing based on years of strong standardized test scores. As a National School of Character, awarded in 2006, 2012 and 2017, the character education program directs a positive school culture of respect and responsibility. The population diversity serves to enhance the richness of the learning experience, tolerance, and appreciation of cultural differences.

The Shades Cahaba Way was born in 2002 and consists of 6 simple rules or life lessons. They are as follows:

- Speak for yourself, and others when needed.
- Listen to others, and they will listen to you.
- Avoid put-downs, who needs them?
- Take charge of yourself; you are responsible for you.
- Show respect, every person is important.
- Have fun, life is a gift!

The Shades Cahaba Way creates a common language among faculty, staff, students, and parents. Having a common set of values is a way to constantly remind, address, and teach character traits to the students. Today, the Shades Cahaba Way is heard not only in the halls, but also at the community pool, in Scout meetings, on the ball fields, at Homewood Middle School and at the family dinner table. The school believes that this effort of building students of outstanding character allows them to "educate, respect, protect and love children."

Recipes

AS YOU CAN TELL BY THE STORIES in our lunchroom chapter, the lunchroom is a favorite memory of former students. I mentioned the peanut butter balls, and I have included the recipe here. There was also a brownie I remember well, and I found the recipe online. I am sharing it as well.

SHADES CAHABA PEANUT BUTTER BALLS

- 2 cups Sugar
- 2 cups Corn Syrup
- 4 cups - Peanut Butter
- 12 cups - Cereal (corn flakes or rice krispies)

Bring sugar and corn syrup to a boil. Mix peanut butter into the mix until is smooth. Pour over cereal, mix and spread into a pan. Cut them in squares to serve or roll them up in a ball.

BEST DARN BROWNIES - LUNCHROOM LADIES 50-YEAR-OLD RECIPE

INGREDIENTS

- 1 cup butter
- 1/2 cup cocoa
- 2 cups flour
- 2 cups sugar
- 4 eggs
- 4 tsp vanilla
- 1 cup chopped nuts

BAKE

- Pour in 9x13 pan and bake 20-25 minutes at 350 degrees
- Check at 20 minutes for firmness. Poke the center with a toothpick and if it comes out clean, the cake is done.

ICING

- 1/4 cup softened butter
- 1/4 cup can milk (regular milk is fine)
- 1/4 cups cocoa
- 3 cups powdered sugar
- dash salt

HOMEWOOD HIGH SCHOOL CHILI CIRCA 1981

This recipe has nothing to do with Shades Cahaba, but I had space and decided to share it with you. Chili was one of my favorite meals, and I missed it when I graduated. A few years later, I went to the school, found the lunchroom manager, and asked for the recipe. She was thrilled to know that I loved it so much, and she rushed off to write it down for me. She mentioned that one time they had a lot of dried lima beans that they didn't know what to do with, so they ground them up and put them in the chili. It was a huge hit. Good luck adjusting the recipe from school size to one suitable for you and your family.

INGREDIENTS

- 80 lbs. Ground Beef
- 6 – #10 Cans Diced Tomatoes
- 2 – #10 Cans Sauce (or paste)
- 18 – #10 Cans Pinto Beans
- 5 lbs. Chili Powder
- 5 lbs. Onions

COOK

- Cook meat until done
- Add all ingredients in a large pot
- Simmer 2 hours
- Serve

#10 cans are those really big cans that you might have seen at Sam's Club and that restaurants use.

Notes on Sources

THERE ARE MANY PEOPLE who gave me advice and pointed me in the right direction while I worked on the Shades Cahaba Oral History Project. I have thanked them in the acknowledgments. I worked on some larger themes that I wanted to tackle and I built a timeline with some basic information. Then I went looking for sources and people to interview. Here they are in no particular order.

It's safe to say that this project would not have happened without the book *Homewood: The Life of a City* (Homewood: Friends of the Homewood Public Library, 2001) written by Sheryl Summe. The stories and corresponding notes made research much easier. I was happy that she agreed to be on the podcast and talk about her book. She would be the first to tell you that her research was supported by Ann Scott and Glynn and Annie Ford Wheeler and many others.

Summe, Sheryl Spradling. 2001. *Homewood: The Life of a City*. Homewood: Friends of the Homewood Public Library.

Additional information on Shades Valley and Shades Creek can be found in the book White, Marjorie. 2019. *Shades Creek Flowing Through Time*. Birmingham Historical Society.

The photos of the schools from 1939 are from the Jefferson County Board of Equalization Appraisal Files. They are located in the basement of the Lin-Henley Research Library.

Photos throughout the book are from The Owl Yearbooks 1922-1949.
Photos after 1949 are from the Shades Cahaba Elementary School yearbooks.
Recent photos of the school and surrounding areas are by Shawn Wright.

Football scores are from the yearbooks and the Alabama High School Football History website located at www.ahsfhs.org. The Shades Cahaba High School games are listed under Shades Valley High School. Where yearbook scores differed from the website, I chose the yearbook as the definitive final score. Shane Paschal, Shades Valley class of 1986, has been working for many years to help compile those scores and I thank him for his contributions to the history of Shades Cahaba.

Acknowledgments

THE ONLY REASON I WAS ABLE to write this book was because of the research and interviews I did for the Shades Cahaba Oral History Project. I had plenty of information, and I assumed it was going to be easy to pull it all together and crank out a book, right? Months later, I am finishing the book and preparing to send it off to be published. Before I do, I would like to acknowledge the contributions of the people who helped with the podcast and the production of this book.

To Don Harbor, a friend who just happened to mention he went to Shades Cahaba and agreed to be my guinea pig as the first guest. I learned how to produce podcasts on that episode. He was also gracious enough to let me publish part of his memories of Shades Cahaba here in the book.

To Herb Griffin, a 1948 graduate of Shades Cahaba. I have probably known Herb most of my life just being around Trinity United Methodist Church and knowing his kids. He is a wealth of Homewood knowledge. We are lucky to have him.

Thank you to The Shades Cahaba and Homewood school staff, Principal John Lowery, Principal Sue Grogan, Kindergarten teacher Laura Estes, Superintendent Bill Cleveland, Assistant Principal Wendy Story, and Registrar Karen Baggett. They have been more than supportive of the podcast, answering my questions, suggesting people I should contact, loaning me yearbooks, and more. I learned so much about Shades Cahaba through their stories.

To Jean Reed Woodward, one of my fifth-grade teachers at Shades Cahaba. Even though she only spent a few years at Shades Cahaba before moving to Edgewood, she has been a great support to me, passing along names and contact information and being a big supporter of this project.

Early on, I asked Principal John Lowry if the school was planning to celebrate the 100th anniversary, and he suggested I contact P.T.O. President Alexa McElroy.

I was lucky to work with her and the rest of the P.T.O. on their Centennial Celebration in October 2019. I appreciate the support she gave me and the podcast.

Thank you, Herman Maxwell, for reaching out to me and telling me your story. Herman was one of the first black children to attend Shades Cahaba in the 1960s, and it made for one of the more popular episodes. Herman was also a player on the Homewood High School state championship football team in 1974.

Shades Cahaba High School students moved to Shades Valley High School in the fall of 1949, and the high school exists to this day, though not in the original location. The Homewood students came back from Shades Valley when Homewood started its school system. I believe that Homewood High School has descended from Shades Cahaba as well as Shades Valley High School. This is the advantage of having your own podcast and book. That makes the Homewood Class of 2021 the 100th graduating class in Homewood, Alabama.

I decided I needed to talk with former Homewood High School principal and superintendent Michael Gross to discover the story of the high school and the beginning of the school system. He was principal during my Freshman year, and I was looking forward to talking with him. He was more than helpful and accommodating. Thank you for talking with me, Mr. Gross.

Thank you, Ken Kirk, for talking to me about your great-grandmother, Ida Tyler, who was a long-time manager of the Shades Cahaba lunchroom. I always had a plan to do a lunchroom episode, so it was surprising to find out this connection to someone I knew most of my life.

Learning about the story of the owl was the most difficult in this series. No one seemed to know the real story, but there was a lot of speculation. Someone suggested I contact Dale Turnbough, she had been a staff writer for the Birmingham Post-Herald and had written about the owl. Thanks, Dale, for helping me tie up some loose ends on the owl.

And thank you, Sheryl Summe, and all the people mentioned in the acknowledgments of your book *Homewood: Life of a City*. If there was a gap in my timeline or a name I didn't know, it was probably in the book. Your book was a huge help to this project, and I couldn't have done any of this without it.

There are a lot more of you out there who deserve my thanks. If I didn't mention you, thank you for your support.

If you are a creative person or happen to know one well, then you know that we are always trying to fill the quiet moments in our lives with one more project. Lately, the thought of writing has been bouncing around in my head, and I have satisfied that craving by writing blog posts and podcast scripts. What's funny is that I was an awful English student. And if this book has taught me anything, I wish I had paid more attention in school. I didn't care enough back then, and now I am playing catchup. If you have found a typo or grammatical error, then it is my gift to you. I tried my best.

I feel I should take this moment to apologize to my English teachers for not trying harder. Especially my teachers at Homewood High School, Audrey Cornutt, Bari Mazer, Kathy Smith, and Jackie Dye. Accept this book as my penance.

Thank you to those that have looked at my chapters and given advice, especially my sister-in-law Amy Wright who gave constructed criticism and sound advice. Thanks to my parents, Rhetta and Leo Wright, for looking at it and my son Aidan who, when I asked him if he could help me with grammar, reminded me that he did have a 4.0 in A.P. English.

About the Author

SHAWN WRIGHT is a graphic designer and creator of the Shades Cahaba Oral History Project. He lives in Homewood, Alabama, with his wife and two children. Shawn attended Shades Cahaba Elementary School and graduated from Homewood High School in 1981. *Shades Cahaba: The First 100 Years* is his first book. You can find out more about Shawn at shawnwright.net.

The Author is on the third row, second from the left.

Podcast

THIS BOOK WAS CREATED from the interviews, stories and blog posts written for the Shades Cahaba Oral History Project. You can find them at ShadesCahabaHistory.com. You can also listen to the podcasts wherever you listen to podcasts and they can be found on Shawn Wright's YouTube.com page.

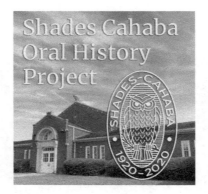